ADOPTION REUNIONS

ADOPTION REUNIONS

A Book for Adoptees,

Birth Parents and

Adoptive Families

by

Michelle McColm

CANADIAN CATALOGUING IN PUBLICATION DATA

McColm, Michelle
Adoption reunions
ISBN   0-929005-41-4

1. Birthparents – Canada – Identification.
2. Adoptees – Canada – Identification. 1. Title

HV875.7.C3M23   1993   362.82'98'0971   C93-093734-1

Printed and bound in Canada

Edited by Sarah Swartz
Copyedited by Jane McNulty

*Second Story gratefully acknowledges the assistance
of the Ontario Arts Council and the Canada Council*

Published by
SECOND STORY PRESS
*760 Bathurst St.
Toronto, Ontario
M5S 2R6*

CONTENTS

Part Three: IN SUPPORT OF REUNIONS

§

ACKNOWLEDGMENTS

This book would not have been possible without the generous support and fearless sharing of their personal stories on the part of adoptees, birth parents and adoptive parents. This book is about and for them, and for all those who have experienced or will experience adoption and reunion.

I am deeply grateful for the love and encouragement of my [adoptive] father; this book is also for him, for my adoptive mother and for the other members of my adoptive family.

To my birth mother and birth father — thanks for being there ... again.

Thanks also to Carolyn Wood at Second Story Feminist Press and to my editor, Sarah Swartz, whose patience and editorial insights are much appreciated.

I am indebted to P.A. Vernon, Ph.D., for allowing me generous access to his post-adoption reunion study questionnaires, and to those respondents who allowed information about them to be included in this book.

To Lisa Patterson and Marian Buchanan: your belief in me buoyed me when I faltered and gave me strength when I needed it. Your love and friendship have unalterably expanded my definition of the word "family."

Finally, I extend thanks to the members, past and present, of my writing group, the Writer's Repair Shop. Your skillful fine-tuning, suggestions and support from beginning to end are deeply appreciated.

INTRODUCTION

The primary impetus for this book has been my own experience as an adoptee. I was adopted in 1959 at four months of age. Like many other adoptees, I had been mildly depressed all my life, and found that my reunion helped to alleviate this feeling of melancholy. I've since learned that some researchers estimate that as many as 100 adoptees for every non-adopted client are under psychiatric care.[1] While this statistic is slightly higher than those reported in similar studies, other researchers have also found that adoptees are overrepresented in psychiatric treatment facilities. I'm not surprised that there are a disproportionate number of adoptees requiring mental health care. The following chapters should elucidate how and why past adoption practices were detrimental to the psychological well-being of adoptees, their birth mothers and, to some extent, to adoptive parents as well. In 1987, I met my birth mother. In 1988, I met my birth father and I have since met my extended birth family on both sides, maternal and paternal. It was out of this experience that I realized the great need for a guide book such as this one. After my reunion, my three-year membership in a post-adoption reunion support group confirmed my belief that a reunion generates many complex issues that should be addressed and shared. Many members of this group were birth mothers, who gave me another perspective on the subject of post-adoption reunion.

I grew up in a large extended adoptive family. Although I couldn't identify the feelings at the time, I now realize that as I grew up, I was mourning the loss of my birth family, my identity and my heritage. While growing up, I only knew that I was sad and lonely most of the time, and that I longed to meet my birth mother.

With each of the many discussions about and references to my adoptive family's "clan," which was of Scottish origin, I wondered about my own heritage and I yearned to know more about my roots. After my sister's birth to my adoptive parents, the contrasts in personality, appearance and interests between my sister and me accentuated my different origins. This added to my curiosity.

While I grew up knowing that I was adopted, it was only when I turned 18 that my birth mother became more than an abstract idea to me. One sunny afternoon, my adoptive mother appeared in my bedroom doorway. She held a pale wooden box in her hand. She was overcome with emotion as she handed it to me, saying, "This is from your birth mother." The box had been given to my adoptive parents by their social worker at the time of my adoption. The box and its contents became sacred objects to me; they represented the only concrete link I had to my past. I wanted more than ever to replace the sparse information I had, and the box, for the real woman who had wanted me to have this gift.

Receiving a gift from a birth family is a rare incident in a closed adoption. We now know that yesterday's closed adoptions, in which the birth family was completely cut off from contact with their child, have serious flaws and negative implications for adoptees, birth families and adoptive families.

In discussing today's reunions between adult adoptees and their birth families, I focus on the experiences of adoptees who were adopted primarily from the 1950s to the late 1970s. These adult adoptees share a number of common factors in their adoptions, particularly the fact that they had usually been adopted by the age of two by a family of the same racial origin as themselves.

When examining current trends in adoption, I discuss children who are adopted as infants, while recognizing that the adoption of older, interracial, international, mentally challenged or physically challenged children is on the rise and, in fact, probably constitutes the majority of adoptions occurring in North America today. I'd like to acknowledge that each of these types of adoptions deserves a book of its own, in order to explore in depth the unique challenges that each type presents.

Post-adoption reunions have occurred as a result of the work of various adoption activist groups, primarily in the United States. Examples are Concerned United Birthparents (CUB), a birth parents' group with a huge network throughout the United States; the Council for Equal Rights in Adoption (CERA) in New York City; and the Adoptees Liberty Movement Association (ALMA); in addition to others.

Through a combination of factors, including the efforts of these activist groups, social and legislative changes, and the attainment of adulthood on the part of adoptees, search groups began to proliferate and the phenomenon of post-adoption reunions between adoptees and their birth families began to develop as well.

With the creation of provincial adoption disclosure registries in Canada, beginning in 1970 in Saskatchewan, the number of reunions sought has increased dramatically. The media has brought thousands of reunions to the attention of the public, thereby also contributing to the increase in demand for reunions.

This book strives to provide insight and assistance to adoptees, adoptive parents, birth parents and the professionals who work with them. Those considering or seeking reunions may benefit from reading about the recollections of those who have already experienced a reunion. Practical suggestions for coping with each stage of a reunion conclude chapters 6 through 10.

The information in this book may also prove invaluable to professionals working in the field of adoption and reunion, and it may also help lend support for better adoption practices in the future, by highlighting the problems caused by past adoption legislation and practices while recommending positive changes.

RESEARCH

In addition to my own life experiences, which are woven throughout this book and in the diary entries initialled "M.M." at the beginning of each chapter, I gathered information from many sources.

As a volunteer since 1987, I have met numerous adoptees and birth mothers, both before and after their reunions. I have listened to the problems they encountered throughout the reunion process and I have shared my own experiences with them. Through this "peer support," I accumulated anecdotal evidence to support the themes discussed in this book.

More in-depth personal interviews of varying duration were conducted with 14 adoptees, 13 adoptive parents, 6 birth parents and 7 social workers in the field of adoption or post-adoption. My post-adoption support group also gave me opportunities to interview many birth mothers.

Additional evidence was available in Dr. P.A. Vernon's ongoing study of reunitees from across North America. Dr. Vernon is a professor with the Faculty of Social Science at the University of Western Ontario in London, Ontario. From his study and its results, I gained access to 350 questionnaires completed by post-reunion adoptees, adoptive parents, birth parents, birth siblings and birth grandparents. Many of the questions required prose-style answers, which also lent credence to the evidence presented in this book.

Working in the Adoption Disclosure department of an Ontario Children's Aid Society (CAS) since 1990, I have had access to hundreds of files on adoptive families, birth parents and adoptees. In my capacity as an adoption disclosure clerk, I used these files to prepare background information for adult adoptees, birth siblings and birth parents who were seeking information and reunions between 1990 and 1993. Through the original notes made by social workers at the time of adoptions dating back to 1918, attitudes about birth parents, the attitudes of and about adoptive parents, and the social climate of the past were revealed. Information about general trends, beliefs and approaches to adoption were preserved in these files. It is clear that the stories told by birth parents and adoptive parents in this book ring true for thousands more whom they represent.

Many articles, books, theses, newsletters, journals and periodicals discuss adoption. However, there are far fewer resources discussing post-adoption and reunion issues. In the course of my research, I consulted all available resources, some of which are listed at the back of this book.

LANGUAGE BARRIERS

Post-adoption reunion between an adoptee and her birth family is still a relatively new phenomenon. As such, there is no agreed-upon language with which to discuss reunions. The use of the terms "birth mother," "adoptee," and "adoptive family" may at first seem unwieldy and confusing, and perhaps even clinical or insensitive. I have used these terms, however, because they are important as they are clear and relatively innocuous. By contrast, the term "natural mother" is offensive to adoptive mothers, who become, by implication, "unnatural" mothers. Similarly, the terms "illegitimate child" and "unwed mother" are heavily judgmental; I have used them in quotations, only to report their prevalent usage in the past. I do not condone the use of these terms. I have coined the term "reunitees" to describe adult adoptees and birth family members who have had a reunion. In the following chapters, I also use the terms "birth parents" and "adoptive parents."

Although I have tried to avoid offensive terms, adoption and reunion are such sensitive and personal topics that it's impossible to use language that pleases everybody. My own adoptive father read this book and found the use of the word "adoptive" preceding the word "father" offensive. He told me that the term hurt his feelings, yet he felt that labelling a "birth father" as such was acceptable.

I think my dad's reaction is both poignant and indicative of the need to consider the feelings of adoptive parents when discussing reunions, even though it is not adoptive parents themselves who experience reunions. Obviously, being labelled "adoptive" still touches a raw nerve in some of yesterday's adoptive parents. With the recognition that adoptees almost unanimously emphasize that their adoptive parents are their only parents, having raised them and nurtured them from infancy, I trust that adoptive parents will accept the need to distinguish them linguistically in this manner from "birth parents." Similarly, I've interviewed a birth mother who found use of the word "relinquish" — meaning the act of placing a child for adoption — extremely offensive.

In certain places, the feminine pronoun has been used but may be read to include masculine where appropriate. By acknowledging that the language I am using will not satisfy all readers, I trust that my terms are at least unambiguous and that with the proliferation of reunions, we will one day have an appropriate language with which to describe reunions and their participants.

PART ONE

THE ROOTS
OF REUNION

Chapter 1

ADOPTIONS
PAST AND PRESENT

I always knew I was adopted. My adoptive parents talked about it, and read a book about adoption to me when I was a child of six. I'm sure in the back of my mind, even then, I knew the adoption book left something out — it said my parents were happy to adopt me, but what happened to my other mother? I always wondered about my birth mother, and whether or not she ever thought about me. As a child, I knew I must have been really horrible, or else why would my own mother give me away and never want to see me again?

— M.M.

CANADIAN LAW did not cover adoption procedures until the early 1920s. Until that time, placement of children was largely a private matter, unfettered by legislation. Private arrangements were made between individuals to place children with neighbours and, frequently, with relatives. An unmarried, pregnant woman would sometimes live with a couple who would become her child's parents; she worked for them as a "domestic." Grandparents, an aunt, or a sister might raise a child whose mother, for whatever reason, could not be a parent.

However, children born out of wedlock were considered illegitimate and did not receive the same inheritance rights. The Victorian era and its narrow-minded morality intensified the negative notion of "illegitimacy." An illegitimate child was considered second class and would be subjected to all manner of abuse — from taunts to torture. Both women and children were considered to be "legitimized" by their relationship to the husband/father. The concept of "legitimacy" defined a person's worth in relation to her biological father and led to the denigration of a woman who became pregnant outside the bonds of marriage.

Adoption legislation was established across North America to protect children from the stigma of illegitimacy and to endow them with rights equal to those of other children. Its goal was to place orphaned or illegitimate children with a new set of parents and eradicate their origins.

Adoption legislation used the phrase "as if born to," meaning that the adopted child was to be treated, for all intents and purposes, *as if she had been born to* her adopted parents. In order to substantiate the notion of "as if born to," every effort was made to minimize, if not entirely eradicate, the adoptee's true origins. Her genetic ancestry was all but wiped out with the stroke of the legislator's pen.

An adoptee's birth certificate resembles in every regard a non-adopted person's birth certificate. On this document, which describes a "live birth," the adoptive parents are substituted for the actual birth parents, insinuating that they have given birth to the adoptee. The fact that this is contrary to reality — that the adoptive parents did not conceive, carry and bear the adoptee as implied by the amended birth certificate — is totally ignored by law.

In adoption, as in other areas, acceptance of social change

comes slowly. The notion of the nuclear family consisting of a mother, father and their children is a dearly held icon in our culture. Any deviation from this "ideal" family can arouse fear and resistance. Yet, as a result of divorce, single parenthood, and other manifestations of social change, many of today's families no longer resemble traditional families of the past, comprising two birth parents and their offspring. Today, step-parents, common-law partners, single parents and gay couples increasingly form families. Attitudes and legislation have not always kept up with social realities, however.

In order to sustain the illusion of an adopted family as a traditional one, "closed" adoption practices were introduced. In a closed adoption, limited information, if any, about the adoptee's origins is available to the adoptee. A relationship with or even knowledge of the adoptee is "closed" to the birth mother, birth father and their families. The birth parents lose not only recognition that they are the child's progenitors, but also all legal rights to their offspring. The adoptive parents become the "legal" parents of the child and their doors are "closed" to any contact with birth family members. In some cases, contact between the birth parents and the adoptive parents has been prohibited by law.

While the methods of "closed adoption" were believed to be in the best interests of the child, today we are beginning to understand that they were misguided efforts, based on ignorance of human development and psychology.

ADOPTION LEGISLATION

In 1921, Ontario passed its first *Adoption Act* and in 1927, further restrictions prohibiting the disclosure of information about adoptions were introduced. Records were to be "sealed" and kept in the care of the courts and the Registrar General.[2] "Closed" adoptions thereby became "hermetically sealed" adoptions. Similar practices prevailed throughout North America and few legislative changes have occurred since.

From time to time, as legislation and attitudes became even more restrictive, adoption files were completely destroyed. The records that *were* kept vary widely in content and quantity, according to the judgment of the social worker and/or the policies of the agency or individuals involved in facilitating the adoption. This hit-or-miss approach towards record-keeping reflects the now-antiquated attitude that adoptees would and should never care about where they came from.

Birth mothers were seldom given information about their babies. Many never knew if their child was in fact adopted, and most received little, if any, information about the adoptive family. Information was rarely provided in writing. This policy further entrenched the punitive atmosphere surrounding birth mothers by ostracizing them on legal, social and moral grounds. The birth mother was effectively "disposed of" once she signed the papers, and little thought was given to her afterwards.

While North American sensibilities branded an unwed mother an embarrassment and a disruption to the lives of the adoptive family, this has not been the case in other societies. In cultures in which women and children and the precious bond between them are valued and nurtured, the concept of "unwed mother" is a moot point. Countries such as Finland, Scotland, France and Israel do not foist a "secret identity" onto birth mothers.[3] In fact, some countries have never recognized adoption, legally or in social practice, dismissing it as a bizarre practice. In these countries, the children of unmarried women are raised within the extended family. Even in North America, Native Americans' practice of adoption more commonly retains links among the birth family members; in most cases, the identity of the birth mother is known and the adoptee is raised by blood relatives.

In North America, however, adoptees, birth parents and adoptive families continue to experience frustration and suffering as their needs are thwarted by antiquated laws. Some Canadian provinces have no legislation addressing reunions and related issues. Records are still sealed for life in most states in the United States.[4]

Today's adoptees are still denied many basic human rights that non-adopted persons take for granted. For example, they are not legally entitled to receive information about their birth from the hospital where they were born, and they are not legally entitled to receive a copy of their original birth certificate, which names their birth parents.

Children of adoptees have no legal access to their parents' genetic history, including medical background. Again, myopic vision has harmed not only the adoptees, but their children. If an adoptee dies, leaving no medical or birth family history to her child, that child has no legal recourse and, in fact, is not legally entitled to birth family information. But this information is her birthright, as surely as it was the adoptee's.

Current Canadian adoption legislation is inconsistent from province to province, and laws are exercised and interpreted differently, depending on who is facilitating the adoption.

Until about 1987, adoptees in many provinces suffered as a result of punitive, patronizing legislation that rendered them perpetual children in the legal sense. Legislation stipulated that adoptees *of any age* must have their adoptive parents' consent before they could place their name in a provincial registry set up to match adoptees and birth family members wishing to meet one another. It was ludicrous that a 40-year-old adoptee, for example, had to approach her aging parent for permission to seek her own roots. This law clearly put the adoptee's heritage beyond her reach, sending out the message that information about her birth family was not her inherent right. When an adoptee's birth family files contained little information or were completely destroyed, the adoptee had no recourse but to seek a reunion in order to learn her birth family history.

In some provinces, such as Nova Scotia, when an adult adoptee was entitled to receive background information about her birth family, this information was given only at the discretion of the "Director" of the program, and it was withheld if "the Director feels that it would be detrimental to the adult adoptee or any one of the adoption principals." This is another illustration of the patronizing attitude prevalent towards adoptees, who, despite having reached adulthood and despite having requested information, were not legally empowered to act upon their own choices.

Largely due to the work of adoptee activist groups and a changing social climate, laws concerning adoption are now being reexamined. Some small changes have already been made. Today adult adoptees are entitled to receive background information about their birth families without their adoptive parents' permission and to register in provincial registries if they decide to seek a reunion.

However, in spite of the hard work of adoption activists and the clear evidence of the damage caused by closed adoptions, North American legislators are notoriously slow in changing adoption laws and ending the unhealthy secrecy involved in the adoption process. While some researchers believe that the burgeoning interest in reunions heralds an inevitable opening up of adoption records,[5] political precedent would suggest that this is an overly optimistic outlook.

Legislation governing women's concerns is frequently the last to be shaped. Laws concerning women also tend to be dictated by the current socially fashionable views of women, so that the laws are buffeted back and forth between liberal and conservative stances. Where legislation exists, it's usually restrictive or punitive towards women, or pitifully limited.

Consider any law or policy regarding women's health and well-being, including abortion, birth control, sexual assault and post-adoption reunions. Although these issues impinge primarily on women, they nonetheless remain regulated by predominantly male politicians, legislators and policing bodies. Closed adoptions have been the norm for so long because of our culture's tacit acceptance of the patrilineal order, which legitimizes and recognizes children only through the passing of the father's name to his children. Because of this deep-rooted lack of societal support for women and children, laws and practice regarding adoption and reunion continue to reflect a dearth of sensitivity and insight.

CURRENT TRENDS IN ADOPTION PRACTICES

Major social and demographic changes have altered the face of adoption. One important change is the scarcity of adoptable infants today. When adoption was legalized in Canada around 1920 (the year varies slightly from province to province), the number of infants relinquished for adoption outnumbered childless couples. In 1970-1971, the number of babies needing a home was at an all-time high. Today, according to a national adoption study, undertaken by two University of Guelph professors, sociologist Kerry Daly and psychologist Michael Sobol, a conservative estimate suggests that in 1990, 14,000 Canadian couples and 500 single people were on public waiting lists hoping to adopt. An additional 8,000 couples and 130 single people were on private waiting lists.[6] The demand is much greater than the number of babies available for adoption.

Attitudes have changed as well. Adrienne Black, a former social worker who facilitated adoptions at an Ontario Children's Aid Society, observes, "The whole of society has switched. In the fifties and sixties it was a stigma to keep your infant. For the last ten years or more, it's been a stigma to give your infant up."

Today's young expectant women suffer tremendous peer pressure to keep their infant, says Black. The popular attitude among modern teenagers is, "How could you possibly give up your child for adoption?" Many women are choosing abortion rather than carrying a baby to term and then giving the baby away to strangers. Another factor, however, is that single motherhood is much more accepted today than ever before.

The scarcity of adoptable infants coupled with a wider social acceptance of pregnancy outside of marriage has given birth mothers of the nineties greater opportunities for involvement in the planning of their child's adoption. As a result, adoption practice, if not legislation, is slowly beginning to shed the rigidity of closed adoptions. More "openness" among the parties involved in the adoption is cautiously being advocated, albeit inconsistently.

In yesterday's adoptions, anonymity was emphasized and legally entrenched. Most social workers actually assured the adoptive family that the birth mother would never reappear. Now, timid steps towards implementing communication between adoptive and birth families are being taken. The degree to which this "openness" is being implemented varies widely from province to province, from agency to agency, and among the various individuals facilitating adoptions.

In Canada, most adoptions are currently arranged either through a Children's Aid Society (CAS) or similar agency, through a private agency, or through the combined efforts of individual social workers, lawyers and physicians who are licensed to facilitate adoptions. There are similarities between public and private adoptions, but there are also significant differences.

PUBLIC AGENCY ADOPTIONS

Public agencies have complex structures and practices which have been established and entrenched over years of operation. Some agency workers still harbour the same attitudes they held when they began working ten to thirty years ago. It's no wonder that change often occurs at a maddeningly slow pace as administrators and pro-change advocates within the agency go through the hoops set up by hierarchies, boards of directors, government regulations and the outdated attitudes of some of their co-workers.

Today's infant adoptions at public agencies are handled by social workers. These adoptions either resemble the closed adoptions of the past, or, as is slowly becoming more common, have varying degrees of openness from the beginning. In both cases, social workers are heeding the needs of the birth parent more than ever before.

In spite of the obstacles, in some instances, agencies have been great catalysts for change in adoption practice. Some of the most fervent advocates of more open adoption policies and legislation have been those seasoned workers, who placed babies in adoptive homes only to witness the adult adoptees' lives damaged by the practice of closed adoptions. These workers, recognizing the flaws of past adoptions through the painful experiences of their grown-up clients, are now redressing past mistakes, for both personal and professional reasons. In so doing, these professionals have become valued champions of both birth mothers and adoptees, and they have the most to offer to adoptive families in terms of education and insight.

The possibility of a reunion is now routinely discussed with prospective adoptive couples in many social agencies. Today's adoptive parents can no longer avoid the issue of a possible reunion or contact with the birth family. Marj McNeil is a social worker who began working in the adoption field in

1968, and who returned to this work in 1989. "The adoptive couples that we are dealing with today are being geared up for the child to be looking for their natural families and told that it's a natural, healthy thing. I think if it were handled properly, people would anticipate it, not fear it," says McNeil. "I tell adoptive couples that some day they may be lucky enough to have an extended family, where they have the two families together."

In her book *After the Adoption*, Elizabeth Hormann writes, "In many adoptive families, the biological family has more than a phantom existence and plays some role in the family's life. A kind of new-fashioned in-law, these relatives have the same general advantages and disadvantages as other, more standard relatives. You may welcome them as part of your family or you may merely tolerate them for your child's sake." [7]

Adoptive parents are frequently asked to write letters to the birth parents, says Black, because "we know that the birth parent can live more peacefully if they can get some sense of these people as real people." In closed adoptions, this letter exchange is facilitated through the social workers involved, with no addresses or other identifying information included. Letters may also be written from the birth parents, to the adoptive parents outlining some of the birth parents' feelings about, and hopes and wishes for, their child.

Today's birth parents frequently have some say in the selection of the adoptive home. Out of a pool of prospective adoptive families who have been approved by the public agency, three or four families are chosen by the social worker. The birth parent or parents may refuse to accept any of the families presented for their child, and ask the worker to present other potential families. The birth mother is also frequently asked about her preferences in an adoptive family, in terms of religion, whether or not other children reside in the home, whether there are pets, whether the family lives in the city or the country, and so on. This represents a complete turn-around: in the past, adoptive families, not birth families, were the ones to "choose" a baby, based on the background present-ed to them by a social worker.

Birth mothers clearly benefit from this new approach. Adoptees may benefit as well, suggests Lynne J. Witkin in a 1971 issue of *Social Work*. In closed adoptions, where little is known about the personality and the values of the birth moth-er, adoptees grew up imagining who their birth mothers might be. In some cases, especially those involving family difficulties, this leads to a comparison between the adoptive family and the imagined "perfect" birth family, leaving the adoptive family at a disadvantage. In contrast, says Witkin, when an adoptee knows her adoptive parents were chosen by her birth mother, the adoptee is less likely to fantasize about how much better off she would have been with her "natural" parents, since a bond had been established between the "natural" parents and the adoptive family. The adoptee would also have some insight into her birth mother's character and values, as reflected in her choice of adoptive family.

On the other hand, participating in the selection of the adoptive family is sometimes the birth parent's way of never finding a family that is good enough. If that is the case, the birth parent ends up keeping her child.

"I only feel good about adoption decisions if I know that the birth parent has really pursued, mentally and emotionally, the options of keeping and of giving up her child," says Adrienne Black. Black encouraged birth mothers to contem-plate all the details of single parenthood, so that they could arrive at an informed decision, keeping in mind what was best for the child. "I always believe that the primary consideration is the child," says Black.

Current adoption practices reflect a far-ranging approach. Adoption is now viewed as an event affecting the participants for their entire lives. This far-sighted viewpoint is evident in the frequent practice of encouraging the birth parents to write a letter to the baby explaining why they've made the decision to give the baby up for adoption. Black comments, "We try to help the birth parents understand that the task of their child, as he or she goes through adolescence and becomes an adult, is to come to terms with having two sets of families. Anything the birth family can do to facilitate the child's understanding and acceptance of that, the better."

Terry Jones, a social worker who has counselled teens considering adoption, says that while the adoptee can gain information about her birth family from the social agency, it's more personal to receive a hand-written letter from her birth mother. And, says Jones, writing the letter to her child helps the birth parent to grieve.

Jones has had clients who have written poems to their child, and one birth mother gave her baby a gold ring with two hearts that represented the birth mother, her child, and their love for each other. Another client put together a photo album of her extended family for her birth daughter.

While adoptees may receive information from their adoptive parents (and many don't), they may still wonder why their birth mother made her decision, and they may remain confused about their background, says Jones. A personal letter or gift from the birth mother helps to dispel these fears and gives the adoptee a better understanding of her birth family.

Another innovation in today's adoption practice is the inclusion, in many agencies, of grief counselling. Jones offers grief counselling both before and after the child's birth. As she explains, "We deal with the loss of virginity, the loss of the birth mother's childhood, and, once the birth mother has had the child, the loss she feels inside. So the birth mother is prepared for all of her losses."

Jones stresses the need for grief counselling in an adoption.

"It's like a death in some sense, but it's not a death. It's harder. Your child is somewhere else. It's not final and it never will be."

In sharp contrast to past closed adoptions, where the birth mother was advised to forget about her child and to get on with her life, Jones encourages birth mothers to feel attached to their child. Jones's rationale is that you can't let go of something you're not attached to.

Seeing her child before the adoption takes place is important for the birth mother. If a birth mother knows her baby is healthy and ascertains whether the baby resembles her or other birth family relatives, this will help to substitute reality for potential fantasies and worries about the child.

Jones also encourages birth families to take photographs of the baby in the hospital, both to keep and to give to the adoptive family.

It bodes well for future reunions if biological parents are allowed to do as Jones suggests. A 1978 study published in *Family Process* magazine by Annette Baran, Reuben Pannor and Arthur D. Sorosky shows that birth mothers who had an opportunity to see their babies before adoption experienced less guilt than those who had never seen their child.

Jones encourages birth parents to visit their child in the hospital. "The child's not going to understand," says Jones, "but I encourage birth mothers to talk to their baby about their reasons for the adoption. This lets the feelings out." Jones believes that this step helps birth parents to make the existence of their child a reality, which helps them through their grief and guilt feelings after the relinquishment. In contrast, many birth mothers in the past were not even allowed to see their baby after the birth.

Acknowledging rather than denying and impeding the bond between an adoptee and her birth mother may have a positive psychological effect on the adoptee's subsequent development as well. Though research in this area is still in process, Dr. David B. Chamberlain, author of *Babies Remember Birth*, believes that all babies remember their birth mother both before and after birth. Chamberlain cites studies showing that a baby gains considerably from intimate contact with its mother. "After all those days of feeling, tasting, and hearing inside the womb," he writes, "babies appear eager to look upon the faces of their mothers and fathers.[8]

"Infants who had as little as 15 minutes with their mothers after birth," writes Chamberlain, "compared to those immediately taken off to a nursery, were found to smile more and cry less during observations three months later."[9]

Public agencies have the advantage of offering care for the birth mother's child in a foster home, if the birth mother is not ready to make a decision while her child is still in hospital. In such a case, a temporary care agreement, allowing the baby to stay in a foster home for a specified period gives the birth mother time to make her decision. In the foster home, the birth mother can visit the child every day if she wishes, says Jones. She can take a day or up to two years to make a decision. They need time in order not to make a rush decision. "I don't want any 'what ifs,' " comments Jones.

Jones does not encourage the practice of placing a child in an adoptive home directly from hospital, as is done in private placements. While this minimizes the number of caretakers involved with the child, the more important consideration, says Jones, is the birth parents' confidence in their decision. "If birth parents have to spend some time in a foster home saying their goodbyes, let them," she remarks.

If the birth mother changes her mind about the adoption, she shouldn't have the added pressure and guilt of the baby's removal from its prospective adoptive family, adds Jones. This would also be difficult for the adoptive family, who would have had the child in their home only to suffer the loss of the baby if the birth mother reverses her decision. This reversal can occur only before the adoption has become legally finalized, and in accordance with the specific legislation of each province.

Dr. Joyce Pavao, a professional in the adoption and post-adoption field in Massachusetts, USA, sometimes arranges to have both the birth mother and her child placed in the same foster home. That way, the birth mother has the opportunity to try out her parenting skills and then to make an informed decision. Due to the continuing closed nature of most public agency adoptions, however, this is not a common practice in North America.

PRIVATE ADOPTIONS

Since 1988, more Canadian babies are being adopted privately than through the public network, according to researchers Daly and Sobol, professors at the University of Guelph.[10] Part of the reason for this is the incredible competition facing today's prospective parents as they vie for approval from public adoption agencies for the opportunity to parent. Finding an infant to adopt can take some finely-tuned detective work and the "right connections." Private workers and private agencies may have those connections, which speeds up the adoption process. Often, they have access to physicians who let them know about prospective adoptable children. Daly and Sobol state that private adoptions can trim the waiting period by four years (it takes approximately six years for public agencies to complete an adoption).[11] Depending on the circumstances, private adoptions can take from several months to several years.

Unlike agency adoptions, which cost nothing, private adoptions have fee schedules. Private adoption workers, including doctors, lawyers and social workers, say that fees for a private adoption range from $3,500 to $5,900. An article in *The Globe and Mail* in November of 1992 suggests that fees of

$10,000 and up to $20,000 are not uncommon. Adoption Options, a private adoption agency in Calgary and Edmonton, Alberta, runs a mandatory weekend workshop for adoptive parents that costs $500. In addition, adoptive parents must pay legal and administrative fees, which add to the final tally of $4,800.

On the positive side, private adoption workers can provide a more "personal" touch to the adoption process. They often work from their homes, as opposed to sterile public agency offices. Private workers' personal perspectives regarding issues related to adoption, including disclosure of the child's adoptive status, growth and development, and reunion issues will become a part of the adoption procedure. It is therefore important, in a private adoption, for the personalities and the values of prospective parents, the private worker, and her clients to mesh.

Another difference is that the private adoption worker or agency liaises with both the birth mother and the adoptive parents. In a public agency, these parties are usually dealt with by different departments. Having one person handle the adoption allows the worker to know each party personally and intimately, and enables her to facilitate a closer connection between birth parents and adoptive parents. On the negative side, this intimacy may also create a conflict of interest, if the worker has a bias toward one or the other party.

Private agencies and workers may be more inclined to facilitate open and semi-open adoptions, as they cater more carefully to their fee-paying clientele's wishes and operate under fewer restrictions compared to public agencies.

At Adoption Options, every adoption has a degree of openness. Birth mothers state what qualities they'd like in an adoptive family for their child, and then choose from the options presented to them. Birth mothers who use this agency may meet their child's adoptive parents, and they may choose to stay involved after the relinquishment, through letters, telephone contact, and/or visits with the adoptive family. One birth mother met her daughter's adoptive parents in their home when she was eight months pregnant, and then invited the adoptive parents to share "their" child's home birth with her and members of her family.

A private worker may have more time to offer in-depth counselling to her clients than a social worker functioning in an underfunded and overextended social services agency. On the other hand, a private worker functioning in isolation might not be as up-to-date on the most current information shared by social workers through interagency exchanges and government training.

It could be more difficult, at a later time, to access non-identifying information from a private worker. While established Children's Aid Societies offer continuity over time (workers change, but the agency remains), private workers may retire, move away or die, leaving a gap in services to their clientele.

OPEN ADOPTION PRACTICES

Regardless of the new trend towards openness and contact between adoptive and birth families, there are innumerable legal, social and psychological hurdles to overcome before open adoption becomes a reality.

As in the past, birth parents today continue to lose all legal rights to their child once the adoption becomes legally finalized in court. This means that promises pertaining to letter exchanges, telephone calls, and personal contact are easily broken. Even if the parties have signed a written agreement, that agreement cannot be upheld by law.

While adoptive parents may appear to be open in their adoptive arrangements, once they begin to parent their child, the fear of losing the adoptee to her birth mother surfaces, all too often thwarting even the best intentions. Birth parents, too, may feel capable at first of maintaining contact with the adoptive family and their child, but they may eventually find this emotionally difficult and withdraw from involvement. In both cases, on-going support from the agency or private worker who arranged the adoption can make all the difference. Education and communication are also important, enabling both parties to understand the position and feelings of the other, and paving the way over the rough spots in this new terrain.

Because there is no legal support for them at the moment, it is not uncommon for birth parents to find that their child's family has moved, leaving no forwarding address, or for the adoptive parents to lose track of the birth mother, who has perhaps found on-going contact too painful. Deeply entrenched fears about the adoptee's loyalty, about their own importance to the child, and about the importance of both families to the adoptee plague these fledgling attempts at open adoption.

Another serious concern is the lack of standards and legislation regarding who conducts and regulates adoptions. Most provinces do not license private adoption workers, and some prohibit private adoption altogether. Procedures, policies and standards regarding private adoption vary even more widely than does legislation governing public adoption. The law has not caught up with the changing social climate, which is tending to support greater openness in adoption.

In both agency and private adoptions, when the workers involved are in step with the current changes in adoption, adoptive parents are being treated in a radically different manner compared to would-be parents of the past. "We're now meeting with prospective adoptive parents to prepare them for adoption as a life-long process," says Adrienne Black. Today's adoptive parents are encouraged to recognize that they are not the only set of parents, even though they are the only pair to "parent." Adoptive parents are taught that an adoptee will experience developmental stages that are unique to adoptees.

Positive attitudes held by today's adoptive parents will not only help adoptees to feel comfortable about reunions, but also, in some cases, their openness will make reunions redundant. There is no need for an adoptee to "reunite" with a birth parent with whom she has had on-going contact, whether it's been through letters or personal visits.

Marian is an adoptive mother who adopted Sarah privately in 1986. "From day one, we've always had a very special place in our hearts for Sarah's family and her birth mother and I hope we can be part of the process to meet her," says Marian. She's been trying to find out if Sarah's birth mother is interested in periodic correspondence about Sarah. Her efforts have been thwarted by current legislation and the attitudes of adoption professionals. "It's as if they'll be opening something that's going to be really, really scary," says Marian. This "opening a can of worms" attitude is an echo of past secretive adoption practices. Marian says that the difficulty lies in not knowing how Sarah's birth mother is feeling about the adoption. And, adds Marian, she and her husband have no wish to "foist ourselves upon her." It's impossible for Marian to find out how much contact is desired by the birth mother since her hands are tied by "the powers that be."

Marian has founded a support group for new adoptive parents. Her openness is not unusual among modern adoptive parents, although it exists in varying degrees. "I know people who met with the birth parent at the time of placement," says Marian. "I know others who are carrying on an annual or semi-annual exchange of letters. There are others who have absolutely no contact or even any kind of interest, because of their own fears."

At the time of the adoption, Marian and her husband

exchanged letters with Sarah's birth mother, through their lawyer. "As a person new to the whole adoption process at that point," recalls Marian, "I didn't feel at all threatened by the idea of a reunion. We gave so much information about ourselves I'm sure if she really wanted to find us, she could. I suppose subconsciously it could have been deliberate. But I think we just wanted to reassure her that we would do our very best to be parents to her child, whom she had obviously agonized over."

Marian considers the possibility of her daughter's reunion with her birth mother an inevitable part of the adoption. At age five, her daughter has already begun to ask about her birth mother.

"I would like to be able to answer all of Sarah's questions," says Marian. "That's why I would like to have contact, I guess. If Sarah's really interested in finding out more information before she's 18, I would certainly do what I could to help her, if I felt that was something that was really important to her. I certainly wouldn't stand in her way. Who knows, by that point maybe the rules will be more open."

While North American legislation is slowly moving towards more openness in adoption, much work has yet to be done to prevent the errors of the past. Knowledge gained from mistakes in less enlightened adoption practices can be applied to help shape future practices and policies — from hospital treatment of birth mothers to placement in adoptive homes, and throughout the adoptee's entire life.

§

CHAPTER 2

THE BIRTH MOTHER'S EXPERIENCE

*As my birth mother and I began to communicate through
letters, adult to adult, slowly, her side of the adoption story
materialized. She had also suffered. The first letter I ever
received from her was addressed to "Diana," my birth name.
She wrote, "Here I sit not knowing how to bridge all the
years. Do you have a beautiful, satiny-smooth wooden box,
with a necklace inside, which was to give you at least one
anchor to your beginning? And did you have a loving home
with two parents? In those difficult days, that was my
strongest need, to give you the home I couldn't offer. I don't
know what to expect, or how you feel about your mother who
had to give you up. I prayed that you were in loving hands. I
visited you in your foster home. No one can change the past.
I gave up the right to hug and comfort you, and show you a
world that can be beautiful. Forgive me."*

— M. M.

FORTUNATELY, today's "unwed mothers" need not endure the
psychological torment that was meted out in large quantities in
the past. While pregnant teens may still suffer stigmatization,

today they at least have financial support through mother's allowance and similar government and/or scholastic subsidies, including student welfare. They can often find emotional help, too, through social workers and other counsellors who are covered by health insurance plans. Drop-in centres sometimes offer counselling to teens as well.

Following World War I, there was a marked increase in the number of children born to single women. Yet this did not make society more accepting of single mothers. Feminism had not yet developed, and women's social roles were dictated by a patriarchal society. Yesterday's birth mothers suffered to a far greater degree under the "she's a slut, he's a stud" sexist mentality, which labels women and lauds men for premarital sexual activity. As a result, these women suffered incalculable damage: physical, psychological and emotional.

Ostracism of the young, unmarried birth mother began almost immediately upon conception. If she told her partner of the pregnancy, she was more often than not abandoned. If she waited until she "showed," she was stigmatized by her family and her community. If she "ran away," not telling anyone in her immediate circle, her shame and feelings of isolation deepened, and the possibility of support from a familiar person was eliminated. The dislocated birth mother had only strangers with whom to share her feelings about her situation, about the pregnancy itself, and about life's most intimate moment: the birth of a child. Yesterday's birth mothers were trapped.

The birth mother's childbearing experience, usually her first, affected her life for years to come. The difficulties and guilt she experienced shaped her expectations of a reunion with her child years later. Because birth mothers were told to "forget" their child after the adoption and to "get on with their lives," most dared not hope for a reunion. Many state they will never search for their child, because their status as birth mother meant that they had given up all rights to their offspring. At the same time, many of these birth mothers fervently wish to be sought by their child and thereby to have a reunion. These birth mothers tend to have a more passive attitude to prospective reunions, with lower expectations since they never anticipated seeing their child again.

Other birth mothers become more militant as the years go by, recognizing the unfairness of the situation that was foisted upon them. These birth mothers may become active in the adoption field, working towards positive change. Many begin to search, realizing in retrospect their inviolable right to the child they bore, and overturning the expectations of both the law and the society that imposed a closed adoption upon them. These birth mothers, by uncovering their past feelings about the adoption, may be in a better emotional position to deal with a reunion with their adult offspring, since they have succeeded in overcoming both their silence about the adoption and their feelings of guilt and victimization.

PROFILE OF A BIRTH MOTHER

Contrary to prevailing stereotypes, the "typical" profile of an unwed birth mother is that of a woman who has had a steady, long-term relationship with one man.[12 & 13] The duration of a relationship between birth mothers and fathers ranges from six months to three years, on average. Whether the relationship was long-term or whether it consisted of a "one-night stand," the inequity remained. *She* paid for *her* mistake, carrying the child for nine months in shame, giving birth in isolation, and finally letting her child go to strangers. *He* bore no visible traces of the experience or its effects.

In her book *The Other Mother*, birth mother Carol Schaefer articulates the typical stereotypes of birth mothers in 1965, the year she gave birth to her son. Schaefer was in junior high school at the time.

When anticipating meeting her fellow maternity-home

inmates, Schaefer writes, "I had my own preconceived notions about what an 'unwed mother' was like, despite the fact that I was one myself. I feared the girls in the dining room would be just one step above juvenile delinquents. For sure they would be wearing tons of makeup, their eyes black and dramatically drawn like those of Egyptian harlots; Pan-Cake makeup would be slathered on thick to cover their bad complexions and their bleached hair ratted into enormous beehives that hadn't moved for two weeks."[14]

If they didn't conform to the above description, then Schaefer was sure they'd be "dumb blonde country girls" whose "boyfriends drove pickup trucks," or "motorcycle molls, with silver-studded black-leather maternity tops."[15]

In actuality, birth mothers during the years 1950-1979 were typically aged 15 years old to their late twenties, and many were young students, some about to finish high school, some in their first or second year of university. For most birth mothers, the goal of returning to school or to their jobs to resume a "normal" life sustained them throughout the ordeals of their pregnancy, birth and relinquishment.

For the birth mother involved in a long-standing relationship, the pain of rejection by her boyfriend was often followed by rejection by her father. The two most significant males in her life abandoned her when she most needed support. This double-edged rejection, when added to the negative social stigma of pregnancy outside of marriage, fed the birth mother's growing sense that she had done something "wrong" and that she deserved to be punished. The erosion of self-image experienced by many birth mothers often left them with an inner sense of shame and guilt, which led to further punishment in later life.

Tina was 15 and single when she had her son John in 1966. At first, Tina was bound and determined to make it work, against all odds. "My mother said, 'You don't have an education. I'm not going to help you.' I had no idea there was any form of help or any benefits from the government," says Tina. "My mother led me to believe that I would be out of the house and on my own."

"Roger and I had been seeing each other for two years when I got pregnant," recalls Tina. "We talked it over and we were going to get married. Once the parents found out, it was a whole different story."

Tina recalls Roger's mother's reaction to her pregnancy. "She met me at a restaurant and had a little talk with me," Tina remembers. "She said, 'I feel badly, but it's up to you to decide what you would like to do with your problem.'"

Rosemary, who became a birth mother in 1970 at 18 years of age, says, "When I told my boyfriend I was pregnant, he said, 'That's tough.' I was standing in the pouring rain, with no shoes on, five months pregnant. He turned around and walked down the street. That's the last I ever saw of him."

Rosemary continues, "My parents made it perfectly clear that there was no way I could keep my baby. My mother never supported me. I had brought this shame on the family. Then I found out years later that every one of them, my mother and her sisters, were all pregnant when they got married. I thought it was so ironic."

Social worker Marj McNeil agrees that, in addition to the minimal services offered by agencies, a birth mother frequently had little support from her family, particularly if she wished to keep her child. After the child was born, the family often wished to bury the incident in the past and forget it ever happened.

Not only was emotional support lacking for these women, but pressure was also exerted for them to make a decision they may or may not have been ready to make. Many birth mothers today report feeling "coerced" into giving up their infants.

One 15-year-old birth mother remembers that her mother

wanted her baby to die, so she wouldn't have to make the painful decision to relinquish. While the birth mother was in labour, she heard her mother say, "Hopefully the cord will tie around its neck and it'll kill the baby."

Tina says she was not told that she had some time during which she could reverse her decision.

"If I'd known that," says Tina, "I think I would have gotten my son back."

On reflection, Tina feels that the legal period during which the birth mother can reverse such a crucial decision after signing her consent to the adoption is not long enough. "If a mother doesn't know what she's doing, it's going to take a month after she gets home to get back on her feet, for her breasts to dry up, for her body to shrink back, and to know where she's going," says Tina.

Rosemary, whose daughter was adopted through a public agency, says, "I had about six or seven weeks of counselling before my baby's birth. There was no mention of my keeping the baby or going on mother's allowance, or that they would assist me. They didn't tell me I could keep the baby in foster care until I was back on my own feet. They kept emphasizing that the baby would go to a better home. They never asked what I wanted. The attitude was, you have a baby we want and we have a family, a mother and a father, who want the baby. They really drilled into me that it was important for my baby to have two parents."

Ursula was 27 years old when her son Stephen was born. A recent immigrant to Canada, she had separated from her husband, who was not Stephen's father. She and her husband had one child of their own at the time of Stephen's birth. Ursula's husband told her to give up the baby or he would take away their other son. "Here I was already with one child, and a baby that I felt I didn't know yet. What was I supposed to do?" asks Ursula.

"The CAS social worker told me it would be better if I gave up my son, since my husband did not want him," recalls Ursula. "I went along with the social workers. I was completely dependent on my husband, I had worked in Holland, but not in Canada, and my English was not that good."

ABOUT BIRTH FATHERS

Yesterday's birth fathers had even fewer options available to them than birth mothers.

A birth mother was stripped of her legal parental rights when relinquishing a child to adoption, but a birth father had no rights to begin with. The exception to this rule was the birth father who was also the legal "parent" of the child, that is, married to the birth mother. If a woman conceived a child by a man other than her husband, she still required her *husband's* consent to the adoption. The biological father had no legal rights whatsoever, having no claim over a woman who was married to another man, or to her offspring, even if he *was* the birth father.

Because of the legal and social contexts, birth fathers were more often than not an absentee party to the adoption or a minimal financial support, at best. Many birth fathers urged the mother to relinquish the child for adoption. Many left the relationship when they learned of the pregnancy. Others were not even aware of their parentage. Society did not encourage or support a father who wished to participate in planning for his child's future. The option of raising the child himself did not even exist. It was even less likely that a man could be a single parent than a woman.

HIDING FROM THE COMMUNITY

Often, the birth mother's parents formed a united front, propelling the birth mother to another city to hide her "sin," and forbidding her to continue seeing her partner. In an effort to avoid parental disdain or complications with the birth father, many birth mothers decided to "go it alone," not telling anyone about their pregnancy. These women ended the relationship with the birth father. The majority moved to another town or province, or even to another country, until after the birth.

Karen, a birth mother who was 20 when her daughter Susan was born, reflects the naivete of the times. Karen recalls, "I believed placing my baby for adoption would disrupt only one life — mine." Karen's daughter Susan, born in 1959, searched for and found her birth mother in 1984. Obviously, Susan was affected by Karen's decision as well.

One young birth mother tried to stay in her neighbourhood throughout her pregnancy and after the adoption. "We were living in a duplex and after my baby's birth, the other people in the house kept asking me what was wrong, why didn't I bring the baby home? I didn't know what to say, so I moved to another neighbourhood."

When she was about four months pregnant, Tina's mother sent her to her aunt in Thunder Bay. There, she was hired to work in a restaurant. Tina was 15 years old at the time, and remembers one of her co-workers making sexual advances towards her. She complained, but to no avail.

Tina says, "Because I was already pregnant, the guy said I was luring him. I was sent home with an even bigger label. I had a capital 'T' on my head that said 'tramp.' I felt like a piece of shit."

Tina and Roger, the father of her baby, continued to see each other "on the sly" says Tina, but "Roger didn't talk about the baby. I didn't have any support from anybody."

"I didn't tell my mother until I was five months pregnant," says Rosemary, who was 18, unmarried and living at home with her parents at the time.

After she'd spent a couple of months in a maternity home,

Rosemary moved back to her parents' house in her hometown. The Children's Aid Society in Rosemary's town found Rosemary a "domestic placement" where Rosemary was to work and live as she awaited childbirth. Rosemary finally left her "job," for which she was never paid, after the couple became violent with one another. The last resort was to return to her parents' home. She was, by now, eight months pregnant.

"For my doctor's appointments, my dad would pull the car up to the side of the house and quickly open the door. I'd jump in and have to lie on the floor of the car until we got down the street, because my mother didn't want anybody to see me," recalls Rosemary.

"My mother pulled down the blinds and the drapes when we got home, and at two or three in the morning, I'd be allowed to walk around the block for exercise."

LACK OF SUPPORT RESOURCES

In November 1985, the Ontario Government hired Ralph Garber to conduct an extensive study of adoption and reunions. In his report, Garber says "The care, opportunities and resources for single parents — as meager as they seem today — were almost non-existent as recently as two decades ago."[16] Therefore, concluded Garber, the birth parents' decision to relinquish their baby had a basis in reality, considering the lack of social resources for single parents.[17]

Maternity homes for unwed mothers existed, but they only served to further stigmatize pregnant young women by removing them from their families, friends and neighbours. Run mostly by religious organizations such as the Salvation Army, or by nuns, or by married couples, these "homes" could create an austere and frightening atmosphere for the birth mother, whose freedom of movement was strictly curtailed by these instant chaperones and guardians. Typically, birth mothers were expected to help out in these homes with chores such as cleaning, dish-washing, and so on. In return, they were provided with room and board, which was paid for by the provincial government and sometimes partly by the birth mother herself, or her family. Infrequently, birth fathers contributed to the birth mother's expenses throughout her pregnancy and hospital stay. While the birth mother's physical needs were met, seldom were her emotional needs addressed in the maternity homes. This was left up to the social worker involved in the "case."

"I was sent to a home for unwed mothers," says Rosemary. "It was like a jail, like prison. Every time you walked out of the room, the door was locked. I just couldn't take it. I felt like I was being punished."

"In the unwed mothers' home, we used to talk about how to get a job and earn enough to support the child," Karen relates. "It just wasn't possible. I had taken a business course, but I'd never worked. I think if I'd had a year of work behind me, I might have tried to keep my baby. But I had no idea how I would get a job, or what I could make."

The secrecy surrounding these unwed mothers was an extension of the puritanical upbringing and lack of sex education prior to the eighties, factors which, in many cases, led to unplanned pregnancies. The birth mother was also usually uneducated in the process of childbearing. These birth mothers learned the facts of life through experience. Young, unmarried and pregnant, these women were forced to grow up fast.

"I was never told what to expect of the childbearing experience," says Tina. "I had no idea. My doctor never even told me how painful it would be."

Tina gave birth to John in 1966. As she explains, "Birth control pills were just coming into vogue in those days, but what did I know about birth control? My mother never once sat me down, nor did my doctor, to discuss birth control. I was just told never to do it ever again."

Hospital treatment was no better than that in the maternity homes. Ursula remembers her hospital stay vividly: "I saw Stephen the day he was born. All the women in my room had their babies brought to them and they kept asking me why I wouldn't have my baby come to the room. I said, 'He's too small.' I had to make up something. I didn't want them to know I was giving him up. I had this guilt complex that I was a bad woman and had done something wrong," says Ursula.

Hospital personnel contributed to Ursula's poor self-image. "I was not even allowed to touch him," she remembers. "I didn't ask to, because I was so scared. I didn't know what to ask and what I was allowed."

Whatever feelings of guilt, sadness or helplessness a birth mother may have experienced could be compounded by her hospital stay. Tina recalls, "On the second-to-last day in the hospital, my minister showed up. It was like God himself had walked into the room. I thought, 'Another one to point a finger at me.' "

"He said, 'I was really surprised to see your name on the list.' He stayed and asked, 'Where is the baby's father?' He wanted to know why he wasn't accepting his responsibility, and he prayed with me. I just sat there and cried a lot."

Ursula says, "During labour I kept screaming, 'I can't keep him! I can't keep him!' The doctor got mad and slapped me in the face."

Tina also yelled a lot during labour. "All I'd ever seen was movies, and if it hurt a lot, you screamed; so I screamed. The lady next to me and the nurse kept saying, 'Shut up.' The doctor came in and said, 'If you want to scream, you scream.'"

Tina had asked her doctor not to show her the baby after he was born. "The nurse showed him to me before they cleaned him up," recalls Tina. "She said, 'You have a nice, healthy, baby boy.' The doctor forgot to tell the nurses. I would have asked to see him, because there is a feeling when you have a baby that comes over you. It's hard to describe and you don't know what it is and nobody can tell anybody else about it until you experience it. I guess maybe it's maternal instinct."

Rosemary was also uninformed about the birth process, and says that her doctor hadn't enlightened her. When her water broke, Rosemary says, "I thought I must have lost control overnight or something. So I went to the bathroom and thought, 'God, this is strange.' I went the whole day like that. I kept getting these pains and I thought I must have had indigestion or something. The due date was two weeks away. My doctor came in at ten and told me I'd be at least a good ten or twelve hours. Joanne was born two hours later.

"The next day I didn't want to see Joanne, but the following day I insisted on seeing her," says Rosemary. "They said, no, you can't. They treated me like dirt at the hospital. I said, that's still my baby until I sign those papers and you have to bring her in. So the nurse brought her to me and I fed and changed her. I made sure she had all her major parts; I counted her fingers and toes. That was the last time I saw her. I was back at work the following week. It all happened so fast.

"I remember the day I came home from the hospital. My mother thought that by buying me a new dress, everything would be just fine. She also bought me a girdle. She hoped that the neighbours would figure I'd been away, and I'd just come back for a visit."

Karen had gone to another province to have a clandestine delivery. She remembers the isolation and the frustration of not being able to share her birth experience with anyone.

"Whether you're married or not," says Karen, "you still think after your child is born, 'I've done this marvelous thing, created a beautiful creature — I want to tell somebody about it!' "

After the initial elation of delivery has worn off, all too

soon reality sets in. "Once he was out of me," says Tina, "I thought, 'I can't keep him anymore. They are taking him away from me.'

"I undressed him and counted all his toes and fingers and he was so pretty, so beautiful, I really did want to keep him."

Even the agencies handling adoptions were not immune from stereotyping and ostracizing their "unwed mother" clients. (My own birth mother asked me before our reunion if I would meet her in a restaurant rather than at the Children's Aid Society offices, as planned, because of prior negative experiences.)

Ursula observes, "The Children's Aid came over to check if I was an able mother. They checked if I had a bed and a proper room for my child. I was, after all, a 'whore' who had screwed around. I was treated like a piece of dirt. Less than that."

After the adoption, says Ursula, "Any time I contacted the Children's Aid Society, they said, 'The file is destroyed. You're just the birth mother and we didn't keep any documentation.' The caseworker at that agency was not very supportive of birth mothers."

Because there were more children than adoptive homes during this period, adoptive couples were contacted immediately, explains social worker Marj McNeil.

 "A home study was conducted quite quickly," says McNeil. "The home could be approved and ready for a child within a month's time. The birth mother came into the Unmarried Mothers' Department, a social history was gathered, the mother delivered and a consent was signed. And that was the end of the mother," recalls McNeil. "She was given very little counselling. Because of the speed at which the babies were being born and processed, the birth mother was offered few support services."

McNeil regrets the dearth of counselling services in the past. "I felt that the birth mother wasn't really given a fair shake," she says. "She didn't know where her child was going. She was given very little information. In fact, if she did not call in and ask where her child was placed, she never knew anything about the adoptive couple." Some birth mothers never even knew whether their child was legally adopted or not.

The birth mother had little or no control over the choice of adoptive family. However, says McNeil, she was sometimes asked what religion she wished her child to be raised in, and social workers commonly tried to "match" the ethnic backgrounds and the physical traits of the birth parents and adoptive families. But there were no guarantees.

After pregnancy and delivery comes the inevitable moment of relinquishing the child. Here, too, the system was hard on women who had gone through so much already.

"When I had to go to court to give him up," says Ursula, "they brought little Stephen in a blanket. They made me go over and identify him. I thought to myself, 'I'm taking him home.' Then they said, 'This is your final day. Are you going to take him?' I turned around and fainted."

While fainting in the courtroom may be an uncommon occurrence, it is not unusual for birth mothers to react strongly when faced with their "day in court." The memories of court experiences further entrench the trauma of relinquishment and add to the painful memories the birth mother must first repress, then reexperience and conquer before (or after) her reunion with her child years later.

Clearly, it is a judge's role to judge, not to be judgmental. Yet Ursula recalls the presiding authority pointing to her infant and saying, "Why did you do this?" Ursula says, "Today I have an answer for it, but back then I had no answer. There were tears running down my cheeks. I never forgot that moment. I had absolutely nobody for support."

Rosemary relinquished Joanne in 1970. "I went to court and I couldn't even tell you what I signed," says Rosemary. "I was out of control, a mess. They told my mother to go to the doctor's and get me Valium for the day. I was so drugged up I didn't even know what I was doing. I had never had Valium in my life. I took two tablets.

"I remember the bang from the judge's gavel—and it was like an echo in my ears and I just stood up and started screaming. I can't remember anything after that."

Tina explains, "The way I got through giving up my baby was by telling myself that I'd made some lady very happy who'd waited a long time for a baby. Some woman took him home and is loving him the way I wished I could."

THE AFTERMATH — GRIEF AND DEPRESSION

Only recently have social workers begun to realize the full impact of the lack of support resources on the psychological health of birth mothers who relinquished their babies.

Soon after the birth and adoption of their child, birth mothers often became depressed or suicidal. Some have subsequently suffered mental breakdowns and psychiatric problems.

Giving up a child for adoption has similar aspects to grieving over a death. Relinquishment, however, is not the same as a death, because the child is still alive. But this fact is little consolation to the birth mother. "I didn't realize that when I went home I would go through a grieving stage," says Tina. "I was told nothing. But when you go home and you've got milk to get rid of, you've got a body to get back into shape, this is a reminder that your baby's not there."

Tina lost a later-born son, Jamie, to an accidental death 15 years after relinquishing John. "I grieved for John as long and as hard as I grieved for Jamie," she says. "Not seeing John or not knowing his whereabouts was just as traumatic as losing Jamie. Every time his birthday rolled around I went into a depression for two months. I can make comparisons to the experience of actually losing a child. The month coming up to

Jamie's death and the month after are really bad for me. And with John, I relived his birth and his separation from me every year." With so little support, it seems inevitable in hindsight that many birth mothers fell into a deep depression after giving up their babies.

"I cried a lot," says Tina. "I barely got through the days." Tina and Roger, John's father, had planned to marry when Tina became pregnant, but they were not allowed to because of their ages. Tina was forbidden to see Roger. After the child was born, Roger began to date another woman.

"Roger was my life," says Tina, recalling how she felt after the adoption. "My baby was gone, and I thought, 'Roger doesn't want me now, and I don't have my baby. Nobody cares.' So I took sleeping pills. I was in the psych ward for a week.

"While I was there, no one ever saw me cry. I had a tough exterior to hide my pain, nobody ever saw it. My defense mechanism to cover my pain was to be flip. The doctor would come in with a wide tie and I'd say, 'Nice tie, doc.'

"When I tried suicide, that's when my mother realized that Roger was a large part of my life."

Tina and Roger married three years later.

Rosemary was 18 years old and single when she conceived. After relinquishing her daughter, recalls Rosemary, "I went to different relatives to see if they'd take me and the baby. I felt, if you can't turn to your family, who *can* you turn to?"

Rosemary tried to put this experience behind her, but "I never did," she says. "I ended up in psychiatric care. I tried to commit suicide by slashing my wrists. I had drained all my resources."

Karen's daughter Susan was adopted soon after her birth. Before her reunion with Susan in 1984, "I had been very closed about my life," says Karen. "I felt that I had a sign across my forehead that said, 'unwed mother.' I was always very guarded about what I said. People like to sit around and talk about their deliveries, and I always had to be very careful not to let on that I knew what they were talking about.

"When my second daughter Katie was born, I lived in the basement for two years and rarely went out. I was so entirely withdrawn that I wouldn't socialize with anybody." In spite of "living a lie," Karen thought constantly about Susan. Karen cried frequently at night, and Tom, her husband, knew what she was crying about. But the only time they ever discussed Karen's grief was on Susan's birthday, when Tom would ask her if she wanted to talk about it. "The rest of the time," says Karen, "he didn't bring it up very often. In March, he knew I couldn't stand it anymore."

Part of grieving over someone who has died is feeling shock and disbelief, and experiencing a desire to retrieve the lost person. Birth mothers report a similar reaction after relinquishing their child. Some obsessively search every stroller, carriage and babe-in-arms for their absent child.

After she relinquished Susan, Karen says, "I moved constantly, unable to settle down or allow myself to develop close relationships. I seldom went home and only for brief visits. I drifted away from my church and I broke off contact with many of my old friends because I was afraid I would let something slip.

"I also had great difficulty seeing my friends because I was so envious. Listening to them complain about their children was most painful.

"I lived a lie, always playing a role, always hiding the truth, and I paid a price for my silence — the stress took its toll in terms of both physical and emotional problems."

Only today are we beginning to recognize that depression is a natural reaction to relinquishing a baby. In the past, women were encouraged to "forget" rather than to work through their grief.

After her baby was born, Rosemary says she worked hard to forget the experience, as she was told she would. Instead of forgetting, Rosemary eventually tried to get her baby back.

"When Joanne was about a year old, I got my own apartment," says Rosemary. "I had saved quite a bit of money and felt independent. I got a lawyer but he said there wasn't a damn thing that we could do, that Joanne was already in her adoptive home.

"I never did forget," says Rosemary. "I ended up in psychiatric care. I went into the hospital after I tried to commit suicide. I slashed my wrists.

"I saw some horrible things in that hospital and I thought, this isn't the place for me. I wasn't in for long. Soon I was right back to work."

Ursula recalls, "I felt very guilty about what I did. My husband would never walk with me in the street while I was pregnant. He hoped I would lose the child. I wanted to commit suicide."

NEVER GIVING UP

Regardless of all that birth mothers suffered in bearing and parting from their children, the majority have never forgotten their offspring. Many hope that their child will search for them. Increasing numbers are beginning to launch their own searches as their children approach their late twenties and establish their adult lives. Birth mothers tend to wait until their child has become an adult, in the hope that they will not disrupt the adoptee's life with the adoptive family. They also hope that by this stage, the adoptee will be mature enough to handle contact with their birth mother. For these birth mothers, the need to alleviate the pain of the past outweighs the risks involved in searching.

"We moved into another neighbourhood after my son was born and adopted," says Ursula. "I looked in every baby carriage when I went shopping. Then for a couple of years I tried to put it completely out of my mind." Ursula later joined a local Dutch club to meet people in her community. "I asked all these kids who were at the folk dances how old they were and when they were born, and if their birthday was in June. I didn't want to make it too obvious, but I never really gave up." Ursula's search was eventually successful. She was reunited with her son 20 years after his birth.

Tina says, "I had pressure from my parents, from the social workers, from Roger's mother, but I guess there was some truth in what they had to say. I gave up my son because I loved him and wanted him to have a home. Now, I'm angry at myself for not being stronger, for not standing up and saying, 'Screw all of you.' But I was scared."

Birth mothers of the past were completely cut off from their children. They also suffered greatly under the bizarre conditions imposed upon them, so it's not surprising that so many yearn for a reunion with their child. Yet, after the treatment birth mothers received at the time of their pregnancy, birth and relinquishment, it's no wonder that many now have difficulty "justifying" their need for a reunion. Many are still completely unaware of their rights under current legislation. But those whose needs outweigh the stigma pursue the reunion and find that there are rewards awaiting them at the end of their search. If nothing else, the birth mother who finds her relinquished baby (now grown up) gains the peace of mind in knowing that her child is alive, and, hopefully, well.

§

CHAPTER 3

ADOPTING A CHILD: THE ADOPTIVE PARENTS' EXPERIENCE

My father told me, "I think the adoptive parent should go in there and talk about the adoption, the earlier the better. But how do you talk this over with your child, when the child says that he or she has no interest in it? You have to find a way into their mind and reassure them. My one great regret is that we didn't get it out in the open, how much your adoption affected you. It could have improved your young life and your mother's, had we been able to do that."

—M.M

MOST BIRTH MOTHERS experienced a great deal of pain when their children were adopted. For the adoptive parents, however, adopting a child is usually remembered as one of the happiest events of their lives, an event that usually followed many years of trying, unsuccessfully, to conceive a child of their own. Adoptive parents were also in the privileged position of being the predominant focus of past adoptions. More was known about their needs compared to the needs of either the birth mother or the adoptee.

There are many reasons why couples adopt. Not all of these reasons are as straightforward as the desire to parent, although this is the most common and obvious one.

Yesterday's morality not only ostracized birth mothers and dismissed birth fathers, it also stigmatized childless couples who were sometimes embarrassed by their infertility. In an era during which sexual and social roles were clearly defined by patriarchal thinking, men felt their "manhood" undermined and women felt their "femininity" threatened by failing to produce a child.

When my adoptive father was 65 years old, he said, "No man likes to think that he's infertile. It makes him less masculine. It's nice to know you can procreate."

For women who wish to have children but who cannot conceive, it can be difficult and painful to hear the stories of others who have successfully given birth. Mothers and daughters, sisters and best friends, often share stories of their labour, tips on caring for an infant, including breastfeeding, and so on. Adoptive mothers cannot share in most of these intimacies and in the bond created between women through these shared experiences. Many continue to feel that they have "missed out" by not having given birth.

Frank, who adopted his first child in 1965 when the baby was eight weeks old, talks about finding out he and his wife were not able to conceive: "Of course we were disappointed, but we discussed it and thought adoption was a good idea. The CAS said sometimes people adopt and then have their own. I think we still hoped we'd have our own children after we adopted. The way the tests turned out though, I think we were pretty sure we wouldn't."

Whether the child was born or adopted, having children

was an expected outcome of marriage in the eyes of both the couple and the community. Procreation was a social and religious imperative. Failing to fulfill this expectation was seen as a disappointment, and a failure of the marriage and of the individuals themselves.

Every effort was made in past adoptions to make adoption as much as possible like a birth. Some adoptive parents even told others and almost convinced themselves that their child was actually born to them. Thus, when a childless couple adopted, the issue of infertility was largely ignored and unresolved. The difference between adopting and creating a child was either unrecognized or downplayed.

Most adoptive couples do not initially choose to adopt. It is usually only after several years of marriage and unsuccessful attempts to conceive that they reach a decision to consider adoption.

Frank and his wife, Louise, were both 26 years old when they adopted Thomas. Louise says, "We tried to conceive for seven years. We thought about adopting in the second or third year of our marriage. We wanted a family right away. We went through tests for a year. Our physician suggested we adopt and said he'd help us."

"We had no success having children naturally," my father told me. "After we were married, we didn't use any precautions at all. We went to all sorts of clinics and doctors. Medical specialists said there didn't seem to be anything wrong. They suggested it was more psychological than physical. We wanted children, we loved children and we both felt that having children was a major component of marriage and of being happy."

There were other reasons why couples adopted in the past. With the emphasis on the traditional family unit, it was not uncommon for couples to "round out" their families by requesting to adopt a girl, if they already had a boy, or vice versa. Similarly, not long ago when there were more rural families, couples sought to adopt boys who would grow up to help with and eventually inherit their adoptive parents' farms. Carrying on the family (that is, adoptive father's) name and/or business was a higher priority in the past than it is today.

THE ADOPTION PROCESS

Adoptive couples had to apply for approval by a Children's Aid Society, by another social service agency or by a private worker before they could adopt. The couple underwent several interviews and supplied medical information from their family physicians and letters of recommendation from family members, friends, co-workers or ministers extolling their parenting potential.

Louise says, "We felt scared to death in the interviews with our social worker. You had to pretty well bare your soul. It's pretty intimidating. In the beginning, you're not sure what they want to know. I had thought that you had to have money, but that's not so."

Once the paperwork was dispensed with, the couple awaited news of an available infant. Louise says this was one of the most difficult parts of the process. "I used to kid all my friends and tell them I didn't have to go through the aches and pains of childbirth. But I think mentally it's harder to adopt, not knowing when your child will come."

The time it took to adopt a child in the past was much shorter than it is today, because of the greater availability of children. "We waited only nine months from the time that we applied," says Louise. "We got a letter in the mail saying that they had a boy for us. I called my neighbour and she came over and sat with me. She said I washed the same dishes over and over.

"I called and made an appointment for us to come to see him two days later. It was the longest two days of my life.

"Because it was going to be a long weekend, they let us

bring him home the day we met him. I wasn't quite prepared. I didn't have formula or bottles. We didn't expect to take him home that day."

My adoptive father recalled, "It was about one-and-a-half to two years after we applied that we learned that your brother was available. We didn't get him that day. We met him in a department store, with his foster mother and our social worker, so that he would feel comfortable. We were delighted with him. The next week he was given to us."

Neither my brother nor Louise's son had visited their adoptive parents' homes before they were moved there. More commonly, however, the adopted child spent at least one afternoon visit and an overnight visit, before he or she was placed in an adoptive home. Each agency or social worker decided how long the process would take.

After the adoptee was placed in the adoptive home, a period known as "adoption probation" passed. It's no wonder adoptive parents felt on trial, given the use of the legal term "probation." This period lasted a number of months, depending on the province. During this time, the social worker involved with the family visited the home to see how things were going and to advise the new parents.

Louise says, "The social worker visited twice, once just after they placed our son and once prior to the final adoption. I was scared to death that I wasn't doing it right. They made sure that we took him to the doctor at regular intervals."

Once the probationary period elapsed, the adoption could be legally finalized in court and a new birth certificate was issued to replace the original birth name with the new adoptive name, citing the adoptive couple as the child's parents.

"I was very tense until the final papers were signed. I was afraid that they could walk in and say, 'We're taking him away,'" recalls Louise.

THE "PERFECT" BABY AND THE "PERFECT" MATCH

The majority of adoptions were conducted through public agencies and these agencies reflected the thinking of the day. Many misconceptions played into the choices of yesterday's social workers and prospective parents about which children were "adoptable." Some of the stories about yesterday's adoptions seem shocking and bizarre in today's context of political correctness and more egalitarian thinking. For example, red hair seemed to hold a stigma in the fifties and even in the sixties and redheaded children were assumed to be mischievous.

Families stuck to the traditional boy/girl patterns of wishing to adopt a boy first, then a girl, so that the girl would have an older brother and the boy would be the elder child. Or, if they adopted only one child and could bear no others, a boy might be sought to "carry on" the family name.

Because adoption was seen as a service to the couples rather than to the children, and because of the high number of available infants, the child had to be in near-perfect medical condition before being placed in an adoptive home. Adoptees with medical problems that corrected themselves before the age of two were usually seen as "adoptable" and eventually they were placed in adoptive homes. Before this, they stayed in foster homes while their medical conditions were monitored and finally resolved.

Children with family backgrounds of neglect or abuse, or those who were of a racial origin other than 100 percent white, or those who had physical or mental challenges often remained in long-term foster care and were never adopted. This was the result of a combination of bigotry, prejudice and supply outnumbering demand in the adoption market.

Not only was a healthy baby supplied, but also every effort was made to place the baby with adoptive parents who resembled the birth mother and her family. Elaine and Gerry adopted in 1950. Elaine says, "We have all combinations of colours in our family. My husband was redheaded, I was blonde, and my dad has black hair. I told our social worker that colouring made no difference." Elaine and her husband picked up their daughter, Theresa, at a home for unwed mothers, and afterwards attended a follow-up interview with a CAS social worker. "When we took Theresa to the Children's Aid office after we picked her up, they looked at us and looked at the baby and said, 'We would never have given you such a dark-haired child,'" says Elaine.

Louise says, "They asked us if the boy had red hair, would we accept him, and we said, 'Yes, no problem.' My aunt was a redhead."

Many adoptive couples requested a child who looked like them, and it's possible that this was a way of overriding their sense of loss about remaining infertile. Obviously, a child who had little physical resemblance to them would be a painful reminder throughout their lives that they had failed to procreate.

Because of the racial prejudices of the time, it was also seen as problematic for an adoptee to be placed in a home of dissimilar racial origin. Although the majority of adoptive parents were given the option of interracial adoption, they would not consider it. One reason was that the couple would be automatically "marked" as adoptive parents by their child's obvious racial difference. This would have caused an uncomfortable situation for many adoptive parents, as a number of them chose not to tell those outside their immediate circle that their child had been adopted.

THE SECRECY COLLUSION

In light of yesterday's closed adoptions and the secrecy involved, it's not surprising that precautions were taken to hide the identity of adoptive parents, as well as of birth parents. Louise says, "Our social workers told us not to put an announcement in the paper when we adopted Tom. They were afraid somebody out there would think that this was their child. They said if we did, not to put in the birthdate. We didn't run an ad, but we certainly sent out announcements. We sent cards that said, 'I'm adopted.'"

Once the adoption took place, the adoptive family was faced with the paradox that although they had not given birth, their child was seen in the eyes of the law, "as if born to" them. At times, this fallacy would prove difficult to reconcile with the reality of the child's adopted status.

"I don't think that we ever forgot that you were not of our bloodline, but it was not something we wanted at the top of our vision everyday," said my adoptive father. "Our friends were very positive about the adoption. We didn't tell it in the community because they didn't need to know. We thought of you as our babies. We'd talk about our son or our daughter, and then we'd suddenly realize that there was a difference. Your brother was so big and you were so tiny, and I realized this didn't look good. So I'd say that you were adopted, but I felt a little embarrassed about telling it. I felt that I was betraying my children. I always worried that other people wouldn't understand how much we loved our adopted children. And we wanted things in our children's lives to be as normal as for any other child."

Elaine says that her family was quite happy about Theresa's adoption, which took place in 1950, when Theresa was eight days old. "My mother made nighties for the baby. My parents were just as anxious as we were that we would be able to have a family."

Elaine remembers receiving no negative reactions from anyone, but some surprising comments from her neighbours who had known her and Gerry since they'd moved in to the neighbourhood two years before they adopted.

"They thought we were newlyweds and were surprised we were adopting. I told them we'd been married seven years already," says Elaine.

In keeping with the belief that adoption varied little from giving birth to a child, adoptive parents, neighbours, friends and family members all worked towards nullifying the differences between a birth and an adoption. Louise said, "I have adopted cousins, so it was nothing for us to adopt, too. It was just like having our own baby. My family threw me a shower, the whole bit. It was a good reaction all the way around. My neighbours sent over gifts. They had all known we were waiting." Unfortunately, this allowed few opportunities for adoptive parents to articulate, let alone recognize, whatever unique difficulties or concerns the adoption might bring in the future.

As a rule, adoptive parents received scant information about the birth family, and what information they did receive was in very general terms. Social workers explored how the prospective adoptive parents felt about a particular child's background history (or lack thereof). It was largely left to the discretion of the adoptive parents whether or not they received this information in writing, or at all.

Many adoptive parents had an intuitive sense of the importance of their child's birth family, at least superficially. My own adopted father said, "I think we realized that although the cord was cut at birth, there remained a tie with the birth family."

Historically, no association with birth parents by adoptive parents was permitted by law.[18] This policy was instituted in a well-meaning effort to "protect" the adoptive family and the birth mother. Many social workers not only assured, but actually promised, the adoptive parents that the birth mother would never be seen or heard from.

My adoptive father remembers, "Our social worker told us we couldn't go back and get any more information. That's the end of the birth parents' involvement in your child's life. You're the parents now.

"They didn't allow us to have enough information to connect with the birth mother, and the information was in very general terms. They told us the parents' ethnic extraction, that they were young, that they didn't have a lot of education. But these things sort of dim out over the years."

Gerry, now 74 years old, says, "We knew why the girl was giving up the baby. I don't know if the birth family even entered into our minds that much. We were more interested in having our child for ourselves."

Elaine, now 68, says, "When we adopted Theresa the CAS wanted to know if we wanted the records erased and I said no. Some day we might need or want to know what her background was."

The laissez-faire attitude about the adoptee's birth family history was the result of several factors. First, most adoptive couples had tried unsuccessfully for years to conceive a child. In the excitement of finally receiving a child through adoption, their focus was on their own happiness and on being the best parents they could be. No one was aware of the importance for an adoptee to have full information about her heritage.

UNREALISTIC EXPECTATIONS

Adoptive parents had been told that their influence would be greater by far in their child's life, compared to the child's genetic inheritance.

"We thought then that bloodline was 5 percent and the rest of it was 95 percent," said my adoptive father, reflecting the notions of many adoptive parents of the past, and of society as a whole.

Popular opinion held that children inherited very little, with the exception of physical traits and medical history, from their genetic line. It was felt that the child would assimilate into the patterns established by whoever nurtured and raised her. Nurture was considered more influential than nature.

Yet, without exception, every adoptive parent I interviewed noted with astonishment that their adopted child seemed to have many personality traits and characteristics dissimilar to their own. At the time of the adoption, they thought that they would have a significant impact on their adopted children, but they learned as their adopted children grew up that genes played a much larger role in their child's life than they'd anticipated. For these adoptive parents, their children's reunions with their birth families only confirmed their suspicions that much more had been inherited than they'd been led to believe.

Today we know that genetic endowment has a much greater influence than was previously assumed. This knowledge derives from an extensive, convincing and mounting body of evidence. While current evidence is based more on observation than scientific study, genetic inheritance clearly has a far greater role in one's life than has been acknowledged in adoptions in the past. Observations of twins separated in infancy, then reunited in adulthood,[19] as well as of thousands of reunions between adoptees and their birth families illustrate the remarkable similarities between children and their birth families.

Adoptive parents of the past will testify to this shift in perception. For many of them, there was a vast difference between what they were told to expect of their adopted child in terms of behaviour and personality, and the actual attributes of their adopted child. Adoptive parents frequently report that their son or daughter displayed mannerisms, personality traits, habits or beliefs that differed from their family's, and, they concluded, these attributes may have come from the child's family of origin. The erroneous belief that an adopted child would "fit into" the adoptive family as though "born to" that family led to some difficulties for adoptive parents, who expected their adopted child to be just like the one they had fantasized about creating.

Without the guidance of a realistic theoretical framework or sound education about the realities of adoption, adoptive parents were left to grapple with the contrast between their expectations and their experiences on their own. Misinterpretations of the adoptee's behaviours, disappointments regarding the adoptee's personality, aptitudes, intelligence level, and so on, and subsequent concern for the well-being of the adoptive family, were common.

In the past, when the adoptee, usually in her teens, misbehaved to the point where she was removed from her adoptive home, the phenomenon was called an "adoption breakdown." Today we realize that, in many cases, the adoptee's disruptive behaviours were a natural reaction to the stresses of being adopted in a closed adoption. Because adoptive parents were not prepared for specifically adoption-related stresses in their families, these difficulties were not "diagnosed" properly as having adoption-related issues at the root. Often, adoptive parents either couldn't cope, or they would "cope" by ignoring the problems or by ending the family relationship.

Another difficulty created for adoptive parents when the adoptee grew up to be different from their expectations was how to deal with their disappointment without ostracizing the adoptee or hurting her feelings. Again, the main mode of handling these feelings was to deny that they existed.

CONCERNS OF ADOPTIVE PARENTS

In addition to these unexpected stresses following the adoption, adoptive parents often feared that their child's birth mother would turn up on their doorstep one day to reclaim "her" child.

It's part of human nature to fear the unknown. And if

closed adoption does anything, it creates unknowns. In a closed adoption, the adoptive parents know little or nothing about the birth mother and so are free to fantasize that she will change her mind. Louise explains her fears: "Deep down I had a feeling that someone might come to the door and say, 'I believe I'm the mother.' I think that's a fear every adoptive parent experiences. When my son's birthday came around I held my breath all day. When your child is young, you worry about how you'd handle it."

Ironically, while adoptive parents may have feared the birth mother arriving at their doorstep, those who have actually met their child's birth mother have demystified the event and, in most cases, have learned that the birth mother, like themselves, has the adoptee's best interests at heart.

Adoptive parents, on some level, may realize that their son or daughter will eventually have to meet their birth family to get answers which they themselves can't provide. Adoptive parents will often say, "I wanted to tell my adopted daughter all I could."

Knowing that they can't give the adoptee what other parents can give their children — a genetic history, a past, the beginning chapter of the story — can leave adoptive parents feeling inadequate and vulnerable.

My adoptive father said, "When you asked about your heritage, to us, it was not a question about your heritage, it was a question about our parenting. It questioned our ability to be good parents.

"I think adoptive parents should be advised about these potentially swampy areas ahead. For example, they need to learn that when a child asks about her bloodline heritage it's not necessarily a threat to them."

But, says my dad, adoptive parents are always aware of the difference, even if it's only in the back of their minds. "No matter how much the adoptive parent loves the child and no matter how well they brought the child up, the adoptive parent will still have some self-doubts. If it comes down to a choice between the adoptive parents and the birth parents, you wonder which one the child will choose. It's a tiny nagging doubt."

Gerry agrees that he had some insecurities as an adoptive father. "I suppose it did cross our minds, what if she doesn't like us, would she wish to leave here and go and find her original parents? I don't think we ever gave it any heavy thought. There was a confidence that she was our girl."

Donna, the mother of two adopted children, had similar feelings when Lisa announced during her teens that she wanted to search for her birth family. "My initial reaction, even though I expected it, was to feel slightly hurt. I felt that I couldn't give her enough. It had obviously bothered her over the years that she was adopted. We were hurt that she could never really accept us as her parents."

OPEN DIALOGUE

Although some adoptive parents didn't tell their child that they were adopted, it was common social work practice to advise that the child be told.

Most adoptive parents understood the need for this, or at least, the inevitability of their child finding out one way or another. Louise says, "The CAS stressed the importance of telling the truth. We were in agreement because there was no way that we ever wanted it to slip out accidentally."

Some social workers recommended books to read, as in my family's case, but most didn't have any more specific instructions than that it would be best to tell adoptees that they were adopted.

"Our social worker made us promise we'd tell the truth," explained my adoptive father.

Many adoptive parents told their children of their adoption when they reached school age.

Donna's husband, Paul, says, "Having Lisa ask questions about her birth family was something I had anticipated. Right from the start we had determined that we'd let both of our children know they were adopted. One plus one is two, the sky is blue, you're adopted. We tried to stress the fact that her birth mother felt that it was in Lisa's best interests to give her up."

Elaine says, "I don't recall very much about telling my child she was adopted. We told her she was special. When she was little, when we were in the car, we'd tell her the story of how she was chosen specially for us and that we were lucky to have her for our own. We didn't mention anything about the birth family then. Later, when she would see a person who was pregnant, we explained that's where babies come from. We were cautious to say that her mother had given her up because she wanted a better home for her because the mother was too young. It wasn't that she didn't like or want the baby."

My adoptive father told me, "We didn't talk much about it when you were three to seven years old. A kid doesn't even think about those serious things at that age. It wasn't constantly on our minds, either."

But he concurred that when he and my mother did tell my brother and me of our adoptions, they focussed on the positives.

"Our social worker told us to leave positive impressions of the birth parent and our reasons for wanting a child. That way the child would know that they had been loved and that they weren't abandoned. Obviously, it's not a perfect path, but it seemed to be the best one at the time. And we followed it very carefully."

Elaine says, "We felt that our children should know from the beginning. I have a cousin who is adopted and her parents never did tell her. Then when her parents died, she was told. It was in the will to tell her and it had a terrible effect on her.

From the beginning, I used to tell Theresa stories about her adoption, and after all, we adopted the rest of our family."

Louise says, "Sometimes, when Thomas was little and he couldn't sleep, I'd tell him where we went to get him, how we went to the building and he was in his crib. He'd say, 'Tell me that story again, mom.'"

Telling an adoptee about her adoption tended to be a gradual process for many adoptive parents, who geared the information towards their child's level of understanding at specific ages.

Paul says, "As our children reached certain points we gave them information about their background. Ultimately we told them that we would turn their whole file over to them because it was their right."

Keeping an open dialogue between the adoptive parents and the adoptee ensures a healthier relationship within the family. If communication and understanding prevail, the adoptive parents will be better prepared if their child expresses an interest in a reunion with their birth family. The adoptive parents will also have a greater chance of sharing in the reunion and can offer their support during the process, thus deepening and enhancing their relationship with the adoptee.

Like many adoptive parents, mine had mixed feelings about my search for my birth family. But my father was very willing for my brother and me to look at the papers they had kept regarding our adoptions. He always told us that the information belonged to us and we could see it anytime we wished.

The adoptive parents I spoke with felt positive about their adoption experiences. My dad said, "I would advise anybody, if they haven't got children, to adopt, even knowing that there will be some problems.

We can now avoid some of these problems, or at least deal with them a little better than we did. I now tend to look more to this open adoption situation. I wouldn't want the birth parent to start interfering, but to be available on an infrequent basis. I think there's a lot more to learn. I just wish we had been better prepared."

§

CHAPTER 4

GROWING UP ADOPTED

I remember being teased at school about being adopted, and feeling humiliated but not quite sure what I had done wrong. And when the doctor asked my mother if such-and-such ran in the family, I remember being embarrassed and angry when she answered, "I don't know, she was adopted." I wanted to know. I had a right to know my medical history, like anyone else. But I didn't. And everybody seemed to think that was acceptable ... but it wasn't.

— M. M.

AT AGE 15, I began to realize that I had been melancholy most of my life. I spent a lot of time sitting in a tree by the river, on an overhanging branch, watching the water below. I wondered why I felt so sad. I feared that this feeling would condemn me to a single life, unable to maintain a healthy relationship. I wondered if it would lead me, inevitably, to suicide. My sadness was not a passing mood; it had become an integral part of me, like the veins that ran through my body.

What I didn't realize was that I was not alone with these feelings. Other adoptees were feeling them, too, and in some cases, to a much more debilitating degree. According to an article by Nancy Gibbs in the October 9, 1989 issue of *Time* magazine, "Adoptees represent two percent of the United States population, yet by some estimates they account for one-quarter of the patients in U.S. psychological treatment facilities." Given past adoption practices, this estimate seems realistic, even preordained. Only today are we beginning to perceive the serious flaws in the practice of closed adoption, and to see how these flaws have harmed those involved.

In past adoptions, reference to the birth family was typically limited to identifying it as a possible source of heart disease, cancer or other hereditary illness. As we are now learning, adoptees need far more than a medical history in order to develop normally. In fact, a lack of comprehensive background information can result in a profound identity crisis, which is common in adoptees and which is reflected by mental health statistics such as those cited above.

From birth, adoptees' experiences differ from those of birth children. Birth children sometimes grow up knowing they were "unplanned." This often translates into "not wanted" in the child's mind — a painful realization. Imagine the trauma of having not one, but two primary families, maternal and paternal, reject you, which is the perception of many adoptees. Also, while some babies are placed directly from hospital, most adoptees live in at least one foster home before being placed for adoption. This causes the child to endure three major separations before the age of one: from her maternal birth family, from her paternal birth family, and from those who cared for her as an infant.

While my sister grew up with stories about her birth — "You were breech," she'd hear — I grew up with, "We brought you home from the agency. You were so ugly they said we didn't have to take you." This was supposed to be a funny anecdote. I had suffered gastroenteritis after birth, and was, indeed, skinny and wrinkled when my adoptive parents picked me up. And, I dare say, I probably was "ugly." But while my parents told this story with pride and love, to my young mind, it only emphasized the precariousness of being adopted. One set of parents had already chosen not to accept me.

I now realize that the need to know the details of one's birth is a deep, primal yearning. Most children grow up hearing family anecdotes of their birth, and they are rooted in humanity through this oral tradition. If they don't hear stories, they may have photographs of themselves as infants or maybe a hospital bracelet or their first doll. Most adoptees have no information about their birth, and the resulting sense of alienation is both painful and bewildering, undermining self-esteem.

Lisa, who was adopted at eight months old, says, "It finally hit me that I wasn't born into their family; I was *put* into their family. It's pretty strange how you feel these kinds of things. You don't really think about it. It just happens."

Being "put" into a family rather than "born" into one has a tremendous impact on the adoptee's psychological development and well-being.

I remember, in public school, I would brashly announce to friends that "I wasn't born, I was hatched." On some level, I believed this. As a child growing up, for all I knew, I was hatched. My reunion with my birth mother gave me an alternative to "being hatched." I began to understand why the photo of my birth mother at the beach, in navy shorts and a sleeveless top, had such an impact on me. The way her muscles curved along her arm mirrored my own physique. Seeing someone who looked like me provided a sense of continuity in my life. On a primal level, life, death, immortality and genetic lineage all resonated within me; it was a profound moment, anchoring me to the human race, hauling me in from where I'd been, free-floating among the stars.

BEING DIFFERENT

Anyone who, like myself, was raised in a Scottish "clan" knows the important role that ancestry plays in some families. At family reunions, Christmases, weddings — every event at which my large, extended adoptive family convened — I experienced the "alien" feeling common to adoptees. My cousins looked and behaved like their parents and like one another. There was usually talk of geneological ancestors. Even though I felt loved and accepted, I also felt invisible and alone. Who could talk to me about my own German heritage? Who knew what I was feeling? It felt like a bizarre charade in which I impersonated a birth family member and everyone played along. Sharing these feelings was against the rules of closed adoption. I realize now that when I slipped into a washroom to lock the door and cry during these events, I was grieving for my absent birth family.

The stories woven throughout any family's history contribute to a sense of identity in all the family members. Usually, these stories have to do with physical things: with geography, with physical traits passed on through family lines, with shared mannerisms. Family trees and books of geneology help those born into a family to feel like they belong. For adoptees, they also reinforce the fact that they *don't belong*. Adoptees become aware that their own background is different from that of the rest of the adoptive family.

Intensifying the feeling of being grafted onto a family tree were the attitudes of the larger society, including negative stereotypes about the taint of "illegitimacy." Terms like "bad blood" gave a clear message to the adoptee that she was not a "legitimate" person, neither a member of her birth family, nor a fullfledged member of her adoptive family. The term "illegitimate" continued to be in common use until the late seventies. Adoptees could not avoid growing up under the stigma of "illegitimacy" and feeling the sting of this term and its implications.

It is unrealistic to think that the negative attitude of society would not be held, in some measure, by adoptive parents who are a part of that society.

When I clashed with my adoptive mother, she'd say, "You say the weirdest things," or "I just don't know where you got that from." I was keenly aware of feeling that the unspoken message was that she *did* know where it "came from" — from my shady and disreputable beginnings. I was, after all, from "bad blood." While this may not have been her intended implication, such a comment made to an adoptee is an extremely ill-chosen remark, given society's past prejudices towards birth mothers and their children.

These comments, combined with the facts that my parents accepted me although I was ugly and that they nursed me back to health from near-death at four months old, communicated the message that I should feel lucky to be rescued from my birth family. Like other adoptees, I sensed an undercurrent in my adoptive home implying that I should be grateful for being adopted.

"I was six when I was told I was adopted," recalls Lisa. "I was happy. I went around telling everybody I was adopted. They told me I was special, that I was specially chosen for them. They made me feel like a princess."

As Lisa grew older and the realities of being adopted set in, she says the "princess" feeling wore off. Instead, she felt different from the rest of her family.

Like Lisa, I also felt "different." While members of my adoptive family were mostly professional or business-oriented people, I was the true, die-hard "artsy-type" in the family, my head always in the clouds, in poetry, music, literature, theatre and art. I had a very philosophical orientation and felt isolated in my thinking.

Adoptive parents commonly had very little personal information that they could share with their adopted child.

When the young adoptee tried to glean knowledge about her birth and her background, the adoptive parents often became fearful, defensive, or denying. The seeds of denial were unwittingly planted and internalized by the child, who learned to ignore her needs, in order not to hurt her parents. The feelings of rejection, loss and pain associated with being adopted often became deeply buried in order to preserve harmony in the family.

The adoptee's questions represent a struggle to establish an identity. When those in a position of trust and authority, namely her parents, deny what the adoptee's intuitions, feelings and observations are telling her, her identity formation is impaired dramatically. While the adoptee is noticing that she has different thoughts, physical traits and feelings compared to those of her adoptive family, the extended adoptive family is busy acting as though she is not adopted. As a result, the young adoptee feels increasingly helpless and undermined, and suffers a loss of self-esteem. She learns not to trust herself.

The "rule of denial" is paramount to closed adoptions. To speak of the pain of adoption is to upset the foundation upon which yesterday's adoptive families were built.

SIBLINGS

One brick in this structure of denial is the notion that adoptees are always treated the same as birth children. While they may be treated fairly in the adoptive family, and loved equally alongside their non-adopted siblings, there can be differences in the interactions between adoptees and their adoptive parents, compared to the relationship between birth children and their parents.

I watched my mother breast-feed my sister, whom she bore two years after adopting me. They shared a close bonding experience that my mother and I could never have had. The similarities between my adoptive mother and my sister in their physical appearance, in their thinking, in the things they liked to talk about, and so on, led them to develop a close relationship from which I felt excluded. They could even wear each other's clothes! It's amazing how such a small thing can make an adoptee feel so left out. But it did. As a school-age child I remember secretly envying sisters who could share each other's clothes. I wanted to have this special closeness with my own sister.

Sean's sister, like mine, was born to his adoptive parents after he was adopted. "When I was growing up, my parents told me that I was adopted and that I was a special boy because of this. And I've noticed that I was special. My sister goes to university and everything she does is paid for, while I have paid for all my schooling. I have to beg to get praise from my parents. They don't ever go out of their way to thank me, or to say congratulations. But they do say it to my sister."

Some adoptees react to their feelings of insecurity within the family by becoming overachievers. Sean explains, "I wanted to make sure that I went through my life and could say, if I met my birth mother, I did make something of myself. Maybe people thought that I wouldn't be able to be a success because I was different, because I was adopted. I thought I had to prove myself. So I did."

I have heard many other adoptees describe inequities in their adoptive families between themselves and siblings who were born to their adoptive parents. One adoptee I spoke with was physically abused, while the birth child was not. David is a 27-year-old adoptee whose brother was born to David's adoptive parents five years before David's adoption.

"My father was heavily into sports with my brother," says David. "He coached his teams, but never mine, and I felt left out. He also talked down to me but he didn't to my brother." David feels that because of this unequal treatment, his self-esteem has suffered.

"I have a chip on my shoulder," says David. "I've been to therapists and they don't seem to do anything for me. I've gotten myself into a great deal of trouble. I've been arrested for assault and I've been abusive towards women. But I do know right from wrong."

Whether real or imagined, an adoptee's perception of favouritism within the family, like all adoption issues, has the potential to isolate the adoptee. This isolation can be lessened or resolved only if adoptive families are willing and able to recognize and discuss it.

ABUSE

Adoptees who are placed in abusive homes suffer the unintended scars of adoption itself, plus the deliberately inflicted wounds of abuse. Just because couples adopt does not mean that they necessarily desire to be parents. Sometimes hidden agendas lurk behind their decision. There are well-chronicled cases of adoptees being sexually and physically abused in their adoptive homes, sometimes while birth children are left unharmed. Read, for example, *Shedding Light On The Dark Side of Adoption* by Marsha Riben.

Adoptees who are abused in their adoptive homes suffer a much deeper sense of rejection, inferiority, victimization and loss of control than those who weren't abused. The normal feelings of loss, confusion, grief and anger are also hugely magnified for these adoptees.

David says, "It's a double whammy. You're not wanted in one family, and then you grow up in another family and it's like they don't want you, either."

Adoptees may be a target for abuse if they fail to fulfill their adoptive parents' expectations. Sometimes these expectations are unrealistically high, if the adoptee is supposed to replace the birth child they could never have. An adoptee might also be expected to compensate for her adoptive parents' unspoken feelings of failure at not having produced their own child. Again, the stage is set for abuse.

Some adoptees suffer mistreatment before, not after, their adoptions.

Lisa was told by her adoptive parents about the physical abuse in her birth home. This revelation was confirmed when she received non-identifying information about her birth family from the Children's Aid Society, 21 years later.

"All my friends said that I was really messed up when I was 14," says Lisa, now 23. "It was mostly because I was angry. I was rebelling against my birth parents and I was taking my anger out on my adoptive parents because they were conveniently there."

Lisa now feels that the abuse in her birth home has scarred her more deeply than she had realized.

"When I was four or five, I had the same dream, over and over," Lisa recalls. "I'm lying in the crib, just a little baby. Faces are blank; there are no features at all. All I can see are hands coming down. I am tied up to the crib, and they start coming down harder and harder. I start to cry and then wake up.

"I was about 16 or 17 years old when the dreams became less frequent. I would have them maybe ten times a year after that.

"I have scars today that I can see," says Lisa. "Whenever I want, I can take a look at the scars. That affects me very deeply. I can't stand seeing somebody hit somebody else, because I guess it brings back the dreams. If I'm watching a movie about child abuse, I'll get a flash of a hand coming down, and I have to leave the room. It's always buried in the back of my mind."

THE ADOPTEE AS AN ADOLESCENT

Adolescence is a natural time of rebellion, as well as a time of searching for personal identity. This search is particularly difficult for adoptees who do not know a living soul who is genetically related to them. Again, support from one's adoptive family is frequently sought and psychological damage occurs if it's denied.

Sean remembers a poignant moment in his adolescence. "One day we were in one of those family gatherings, looking at old pictures. I said something to my adoptive parents about the fact that I'm adopted, and they said to me, 'If you ever decide to search, you won't be our son.' I thought, 'What are you talking about? It's not your call, not your judgment to tell me what I can and can't do.' You know that rebel stage when you're 15. But it really hurt my feelings."

Adoptees deal with the usual adolescent dilemmas, but also face the frightening prospect that they don't have any clues to how they are likely to grow and develop. I remember wondering if I was going to be thin or large, short or tall. Birth children take for granted the security provided by having access to a blueprint of their growth — their family. Adoptees have no such advantage. This lack of information magnifies the inherent loneliness of adolescence.

Many factors can coalesce to wipe out the adoptee's birth history. In my case, friends and strangers corroborated by pointing to me and saying, "You look so much like your [adoptive] mother." I wanted to scream, "But look at my blue eyes! Hers are hazel. And look at her large bones! My frame is small. Isn't anybody looking at me? What's going on?" It felt like a denigration, a murder of my birth family, a denial that they ever existed. Here I was, trying to establish who I was, and friends and family were making observations like this, which only served to confuse the issue. I felt annihilated.

I wanted to know, and wasn't sure if I ever would know, if I did resemble my birth mother. People were so busy emphasizing how much I looked like my adoptive mother, I felt completely traitorous in my need to know if I really *did* look like my mother — my birth mother. Although I realized people meant well by their comments, these comparisons to my adoptive mother left me feeling selfish, ungrateful and unstable in my wish to find my birth mother.

Sean says, "Everybody always told me I looked like my adoptive father — but I didn't."

My adolescence was also marked by "smelling" different from my adoptive family. The "chemical attraction" we hear about that leads lovers to fall madly for each other backfired in my case; my adoptive mother was repelled by my emerging adolescent bouquet. She repeatedly told me I smelled awful. I scrubbed until I was raw, but she would accuse me of not washing, and off I would go again, in tears, to work my tender flesh to hamburger. I "ruined" all my clothes, and was obviously doing this deliberately to torment my mother. I felt bewildered, rejected and alienated. My adopted mother was frustrated and worried that I would be ostracized by others. I began to worry also, embarrassed just to sit in a classroom.

Fifteen years later, after my reunion, I finally learned the cause of this dilemma — genetics, not hygiene. My birth family smelled like me! I resented my adoptive mother for not believing me in the first place, and for not accepting me as I was.

My self-esteem was badly bruised by this experience. Even in my thirties, I still suffered the effects. I bought a silk blouse, but for months was too afraid to wear it because I thought I'd "ruin" it. What was "ruined" was my self-confidence. Given a closed adoption, how easy it was to "forget" that I had come from a different clan and that families do have their own individual smells, mannerisms and quirks that are not wiped out by a paper that legalizes the adoption.

ANGER

Although I was not abused by my birth family, I was angry at having been "rejected" by them. I directed my inarticulate anger towards my adoptive mother. My inability to discover the source of my anger contributed to an impasse between my adoptive mother and me, which remained, sadly, until her death.

While my anger was obvious to me and to my adoptive parents, there were no support systems or counsellors at the time of my adoption, in 1959, who were capable by virtue of training or experience to help us uncover the reason behind it. Therapists well-versed in adoption issues continue to be scarce, because specific training is not provided. In fact, adoption myths were still alive and well while I was growing up, so that discussion was discouraged, not encouraged.

David, like some other adoptees, began using drugs to bury his feelings. "Drugs are a temporary escape from reality. But you've got to come down sometime and then reality is there in your face," he comments.

David saw a psychiatrist four or five years ago. "He said, 'Take some antidepressants and you'll be fine.' I took two and then threw them out. You can't function on them. I stopped seeing him."

Before this experience, David had seen a psychologist for anger management. "I explained to him about my adoption and that I had gotten into drugs pretty heavily for a while," David recalls. "I told him that I'd met my birth family and he just said, 'Oh, well.' He didn't think it was a big deal. He didn't even ask me anything about it. He really didn't get to the root of the problem, which I feel is a combination of my relationship with the father I grew up with and being adopted."

The culmination of these strong, yet sometimes buried feelings leads many adoptees to experience a vague or pronounced depression that permeates their lives. Some teenage adoptees attempt suicide; some consider it. Many act out in various ways to escape their anger and sadness.

RECLAIMING YOUR BIRTHRIGHT

Most adoptees learn their birth name for the first time when they are in their late teens, when they've gathered enough courage to look for it, and when they feel a desperate need to discover who they really are. Once the adoptee discovers her original identity, she begins to feel empowered. With a birth name, one can begin a search for one's birth mother. Once an adoptee has knowledge of her birth name, she also has a past. The process of beginning to feel "normal" instead of "different" has begun, and with it come positive feelings such as being more in control of one's life. The road to healing begins.

A letter from the Metropolitan Toronto Children's Aid Society to my adoptive parents, written right after I was adopted, read: "It will now be possible to secure a Birth Certificate for your child in the new name at the Department of Vital Statistics, at a cost of one dollar."

One dollar! My identity sold for one dollar! For one dollar, my original name was discarded and a new one substituted. I felt completely indignant when I read, at 17 years of age, how easily my birth name had been swept away.

Sean was 22 years old when he found a document with his birth name on it. Sean's adoptive parents were not at home when he stumbled on this treasure. "I knew I was adopted. But it's a whole different thing being told you are adopted, to finding that piece of paper that confirms it. It hit me pretty hard. It took me a couple of days to say anything, even to my girlfriend. I didn't know how to take it or what to do, so I just let myself think about it and try to understand what exactly I'd just found and how everything tied in."

Once an adoptee knows his or her birth name, realization begins to sink in that the birth family is every bit as real and human as the adoptive family. "It's like two parallel worlds," says Sean. "You've got your birth mother and your birth name on the one side; but your other world that you've lived in for so long is still a part of you, too. It's as if you're a spy or something and you have two lives. It made me want to check into my past." Sean, like many adoptees, used his birth name as a starting point in a search for his birth mother.

It is a quantum leap for adoptees to realize that knowledge of their background is their *birth right*. This has not traditionally been the attitude of adoptive parents, social workers or birth parents, and is not reflected in social custom or legislation. Adoptees, through closed adoption practices, were encouraged to believe themselves to be no different from biological members of their families. Yet this has merely further confused the adoptee, who is already struggling with identity issues.

In his 1985 report, Ralph Garber wrote, "Illegitimacy was so severe a stigma, that only by being born anew with a new set of parents and an altered and 'fraudulent' birth certificate ... could the stigma be hidden. It was never erased." This practice, like all other closed adoption practices, eroded the psychological health of all concerned by reinforcing denial instead of acceptance of reality.

While this practice was an effort to achieve psychological security in the adoptee and acceptance of the adoptee by the adoptive family, in many cases it unfortunately had the opposite effect. The legal clause used to entrench adoptees in their adoptive homes as equal members is: "as if born to" the adoptive family. This phrase belies the fact that being adopted is different from being born into a family. The birth family cannot simply be removed from the child without considerable pain and a subsequent need for healing. The unrealistic expectations of the adoptee to somehow become a birth family member and to behave and think in a manner that conforms to that of the adoptive family paves the way for conflict or rejection by the adoptive family.

Given the realities of closed adoptions, it's no wonder that the phenomenon of reunions is becoming widespread throughout North America. With education, sensitivity and insight into the past, adoptees who experience reunions can look forward to a much more positive future and go far in resolving the emotional difficulties of their adoptions.

§

CHAPTER 5

THE CHALLENGE OF REUNIONS

My heart pulsed double-time as I entered the tiny Canada Post outlet. I held the registered mail notice in my hands as the clerk found my name on the register. By the time he'd found it, the notice was curled and disintegrated at the edges where my warm, sweating hands had nervously bent it over and over.

I tore the letter open and yelled excitedly when I'd skimmed it. The only line that mattered read, "The name of your birth mother has been entered in the Adoption Disclosure Register."

As I drove home, my elation raced into fear, back to joy, then jumped to terror. I was, in short, a mess.

—M. M.

WITH EACH DECADE in North America, new social developments occur. The feminist movement took hold in the seventies, the "me" generation stormed the eighties, and the 1990s may be the era of the reunion, as adoptees and birth mothers break out of their "closets."

Adoptees have huddled fearfully, in secret, with their need to know their background history, which has shaped not only their bodies, but also their minds and characters. Many adoptees share their closets with the ghost of guilt. This guilt stems from not accepting ignorance of their past, from considering a course of action that will "disrupt" the lives of others, and from "betraying" their adoptive parents by searching for their birth parents.

Birth mothers are often imprisoned by their own guilt and by grief, if they have not resolved their feelings about the adoption. The birth mother may have developed psychological difficulties after she turned her baby over. Feelings of low self-esteem, hopelessness, helplessness and inadequacy may persist until she meets her son or daughter.

WHY REUNIONS?

Reunions provide the best opportunity for an adoptee to learn about her birth family, and for the birth family to learn if the missing member of their clan has survived and flourished.

Until very recently, an adoptee's desire for information about her birth family was seen by many as abnormal — a sign of pathology caused either by a flaw in the adoptee, by a failure of the adoptive parents' parenting, or by both. This attitude ignores the powerful factors that motivate adoptees to search: they are curious and anxious about their background and they feel different throughout their childhood. Sometimes they are stigmatized by their peers and their elders, and they may even receive unequal treatment within adoptive families. And always, the experience of growing up adopted is clearly different from the experience of growing up in one's birth family. The quest to "validate" one's existence by seeking one's "roots" is a basic human need, and a fundamental right. Only now are we learning that trying to erase a child's entire genetic lineage complicates, rather than simplifies, the lives of adoptees. Acknowledging this fact is the first step towards healing the wounds caused by yesterday's closed adoptions.

Pursuing a reunion is the next logical step. Because so little information about their birth families was provided to adoptees, many adoptees have no choice but to find their birth family members in order to retrieve information about themselves and their past. It is slowly being recognized that it's acceptable — and perhaps even necessary — for adoptees to conduct a search.

The quest for one's birth relatives gives the adoptee an opportunity to contemplate how she feels about her adoption honestly, and to explore her feelings with a social worker or with a supportive family member, friend or another adoptee. This is a rare opportunity, since adoption is seldom discussed in adoptive families and is never dealt with in an educational context. Feelings about being adopted are often repressed; most adoptees simply do not talk about their adoption experience. With a reunion pending, an adoptee will pause to consider how her reunion might alter her feelings about being adopted.

Reunions can sometimes compensate for adoptees' lack of self-confidence and the feeling of being "different." After my own reunion, for example, whenever I was with my adoptive family at one of our family gatherings, I found that I felt much more calm and settled among my adopted relatives. The melancholy of the past gradually evaporated. I now knew that my birth mother was slender, like me. We share the same wave in our hair and the same bump midway down our nose. Having her image in my mind helped me to feel less alienated from my adoptive family, as I now had my own personal context and genetic heritage as a counterbalance.

My reunion also gave me the experience of being completely accepted by my birth mother and her family. This acceptance contrasted with my early childhood feelings of rejection by my birth mother, and ostracism from other children for being adopted. While a reunion does not necessarily ease the hurt of these early experiences, it does help to make the pain fade over time.

For a birth mother, reunions provide an opportunity to resolve her grief over losing her child and to find out her child's fate after her relinquishment. Many birth mothers discovered that no matter how many subsequent children they had, they could never replace the one they had given up for adoption. By locating her missing child, a reunion allows a birth mother to feel more complete. It also gives her an opportunity to tell the adoptee her side of the adoption story.

Today's reunitees are pioneers, their enthusiasm, courage and need propelling them into the unknown. When we examine closed adoptions, it is easy to understand why so many participants are now seeking to rectify the adoption experience and to heal the wounds caused by this practice, by means of a reunion.

THE REUNION PARADOX: PAIN AND GROWTH

A reunion brings home the reality of the past. Reunions transform the adoptee's fantasies of her birth family into the reality of living, breathing human beings. The adoptee must finally grapple with the fact that her birth family has been absent for her entire childhood, that years have passed that cannot be recovered. No matter how positive her adoption has been, feelings of grief, loss and anger may surface. The reunion may uncover deeply repressed memories and strong feelings about being adopted. Ironically, if an adoptee really *likes* her birth family, her grief and sense of loss can be that much deeper.

Before my reunion, I coped by trying to focus on the positives in my life. I summed up my accomplishments and gave myself credit for having managed in spite of my on-going low-grade depression. It wasn't until three years after my reunion that, finally, my own dam of repression burst. The flood of tears lasted for days.

I had asked my birth mother and father, who had not married, for a photograph of the three of us together. This photo captured the first occasion we'd ever been together, since the time I was in utero. I thought, naively, that I merely wanted what most other kids grew up with, a family picture. Then, abruptly, this understanding was turned inside out.

The "family photograph" of my birth parents and me suddenly seemed like a bitter joke. I asked myself, "What am I doing? Trying to recapture an unlived past?" I realized that on a deep level, I was trying to do just that. I suddenly wanted to say to my birth parents, "Forget the photo. You can't give back what you've already taken away."

A child's anger began to surface. For the next three days, I found myself flooded by vivid childhood memories. I fell into a deep, black hole. I was overwhelmed by my recollections and by the feelings that they evoked.

Before my reunion, I thought all I wanted was information. Now, I was enraged. My belief that adoptees aren't angry with birth parents, that they are just looking for answers, no longer rang true. I sought counselling, and began to tame this torrent of emotions.

Repression takes a high toll, wearing you down psychologically, emotionally and, finally, physically. I began to feel the exhaustion that comes with struggling to sustain a semblance of normalcy. At this point, I realized that the preceding month's battery of physical ailments, unusual for me, was my body's expression of my inner psychological state. I was breaking down, inside and out.

As I journeyed into my past, my birth mother's experience also came into focus. Her choices had been to lose me to adoption, or to marry my birth father and raise me — and be banished from her family. She couldn't bear to give up her family, so I had to give up mine.

Until these insights emerged, I could find no way to break free of my dark, chronic melancholy. Finally, with these revelations, some light began to penetrate. Buried emotions bubbled to the surface, and I felt both enormous anguish as well as a new sense of freedom. My new-found insights, while incredibly painful, were also a revelation, an awakening.

As adoptees enter into reunions, adoption myths are finally shattered. Just as my reunion was followed by three years with no major trauma, so too, will other reunitees experience their reunion as a "honeymoon" until they hit "the Wall." But only after crashing through this wall of deception, repression and denial, does one's life as an adoptee begin to make sense. Healing takes place only after the adoptee is allowed to express the anger and sorrow of her childhood losses; then a healthy, whole adult can emerge.

And so, the reunion paradox: pain and growth happen together. The possibility of unearthing powerful, repressed emotions shouldn't stop anybody from seeking a reunion. The birth mother who refuses a reunion out of fear of her child's anger is missing an opportunity for personal growth. The adoptee who avoids a reunion is also losing a chance for deeper self-knowledge and understanding, as well as the opportunity to have siblings, aunts, uncles and other family members whom she may grow to cherish and to love.

CHALLENGES FOR BIRTH MOTHERS

Before a birth mother seeks the benefits of a reunion, she must face her own unique challenges. First, she must overcome the belief, set in motion at the time of the closed adoption, that she would never see her child again. Some birth mothers relinquished their son or daughter with the strong hope that they *would* see them again, in spite of what they were led to assume by their social workers and their families. The prospect of seeing their child again gave them the courage to relinquish their child to strangers, and their faith in a reunion sustained them in the years to come. But most birth mothers believed the social workers, the legal system and society when they were told they must get on with their lives and forget about the adoptee. It takes great strength and perseverance to reverse this strong advice and to pursue a reunion.

Once a birth mother convinces herself that she may see her child again, she must then overcome her feelings of guilt for wanting to. When she gave birth to her child, she was punished with the message that she was a "bad girl." It's a great challenge for a birth mother not to fall into old feelings of being "bad" all over again when she decides to search for her child.

When a birth mother has decided to pursue a reunion, she will remember that at the time of the adoption she had little or no support. It will be another challenge, now, for her to reach out and trust someone to support her through her search and reunion. She must decide whether she can risk sharing this experience, or whether she will go it alone for fear of reliving the ostracism, rejection, lack of support and subsequent pain associated with the adoption.

Once a birth mother has made the decision to search, she will also encounter practical hurdles. Many birth mothers never knew if their child was ever in fact adopted, and most have little, if any, information about the adoptive family. Rarely was information provided in writing. Most birth mothers don't know that this information is available from the agency that handled the adoption, or, if it was a private adoption, through the provincial ministry overseeing adoptions. Now that they are legally entitled to it, many birth mothers, understandably, do not feel comfortable asking for information about their relinquished children.

If a birth mother has a close and trusting relationship with a loving friend, family member and/or therapist, she will find these haunting feelings from the past easier to overcome. A solid support system will help guide her into the future, whatever it may hold. She will also have the confidence necessary to enable her to approach the agency where she relinquished her child and/or a search organization, in order to take the steps required to initiate her search.

CHALLENGES FOR ADOPTIVE PARENTS

Although the reality is that adoptive family relationships remain the same or improve as a result of a reunion, most adoptive parents remain fearful of reunions. After all, reunions erode the very foundation of secrecy upon which yesterday's adoptions were built.

Social workers Lou Stoneman, Jan Thompson and Joan Webber studied 22 reunited pairs of adoptees and birth families in 1980. These researchers and others found that adoptive parents see themselves as having the most to lose by a reunion. They point out that although adoptees repeatedly assure them that they are still the "real" parents, after the reunion adoptive parents can no longer go on pretending that they are the "only" parents.[20]

Besides the feelings associated with not being their child's "only" parents, unexpressed grief over infertility, lack of acceptance of the birth family as real people rather than an abstract concept and fear of being replaced by the birth parents are among the factors that threaten the adoptive parents' security.

The adoptive parents quoted in this book were all informed about the reunion by the adoptee. They showed varying levels of apprehension while supporting their son or daughter's decision. Many adoptive parents whose now-grown children are having reunions, however, are not supportive of a reunion or are not told about a reunion by their adopted son or daughter. Some adoptive parents did not tell their child about their adoption, and thus have eliminated the possibility of ever having to deal with the birth family's existence.

Because of these issues, the adoptive parent is frequently an absentee party to today's reunions, either by choice, or because the adoptee has not shared their reunion with their adoptive parents, knowing that the reaction will be negative. Adoptive parents who do welcome a reunion will have to confront their own fears and personal issues in order to become comfortable with the impending changes in their own lives and in the life of their adopted son or daughter.

DIVIDED LOYALTIES FOR THE ADOPTEE

The decision not to tell their adoptive parents about their search and/or reunion reflects adoptees' divided loyalties. It's no wonder, given the old "rules" of secrecy, that many adoptees are extremely protective of their adoptive parents while they pursue their own need for a reunion, just as they themselves were "protected" from contact with their birth families. Maybe we've all been too busy "protecting" each other.

Ironically, some adoptees who hide their reunions do so for the same reasons that their birth mothers hid their pregnancies years before. They are afraid of being stigmatized or criticized, and fear that they will hurt their families.

Today's adoptees continue to cloak their questions about reunions in an apologetic, guilty, self-abasing robe, one they donned during childhood. Even today, with reunions becoming more popular, adoptees continue to use furtive, anxious tones when they plead, "You won't tell my adoptive parents I've called, will you?"

Some adoptees feel they must justify their requests for information. I frequently hear the statement, "I'm just looking for medical information." Adoptees' divided loyalties are revealed by their need to explain their requests and to justify their natural curiosity. Adoptees are often quick to point out that they are not looking for a new set of parents. At age 27 — the average age at which an adoptee requests information about her birth family and/or a reunion — who wants new "parents" anyway? By this time, surely most of the parenting has been completed.

Sean says, "My adoptive parents have no idea that I found any information at all. They wouldn't tell me anything. They were totally against my having anything to do with searching for my birth parents. They said 'We don't ever want to hear you talk about it.'"

Because of experiences like these, or the unspoken messages that many adoptees receive, adoptees often have feelings of guilt and inner conflict. As I grew up, my adoptive parents told me that they had kept documents from the Children's Aid Society and my adoptive father said I could look at them if I wished. It was several years after I had received his permission to do so that I finally did look at the papers. But I waited until my parents were out, and, even with my dad's permission, my palms were sweating. I didn't want them to come home and "catch" me. I was about 17 at the time. I still felt a lot of guilt, as though there was something morally wrong with my actions.

Some of these feelings arose from the knowledge that my adoptive mother would have preferred that I hadn't shown this interest, and I knew she didn't want me to look at my adoption papers. She made it very clear that they belonged to my father and her, not to me. I remember my dad saying, "Go ahead," and the look she gave him that said, "Why did you say that?" I got the message, even if he didn't.

I waited until my adoptive mother died before I registered at the provincial adoption disclosure registry, because I believed she would be hurt by my actions. After I received notice that my birth mother had also registered at the adoption disclosure registry, I again experienced guilt. When the notice came, I felt I was betraying my adoptive mother's memory. Many adoptees, like myself, wait until one or both adoptive parents are deceased before beginning their search for their birth family.

THE RESTORATIVE POWERS OF REUNIONS

Reunions are here to stay. In my work at a Children's Aid Society, I have spoken with hundreds of adoptees who asked if I could help them to find their birth family. Yet outdated attitudes linger as a result of a lack of education. In 1993, some adoptive parents, social work students and members of the public suggested that reunions represent a social problem. This attitude demonstrates the urgent need for education in this field. Contrary to the notion that adoptees who search for their birth families are psychologically troubled or suffered difficult adoptions, adoptees in quest of information or reunions usually say that their adoptions were "good" or "very happy." Even so, the very nature of closed adoptions creates a need for personal growth, healing and integration on the part of yesterday's adoptees and their birth mothers. We're just beginning to acknowledge the pain caused to birth mothers, adoptees and adoptive families by the practice of closed adoptions.

The adoptee or birth family member seeking reunion must battle old thinking, just as do gay activists, incest survivors, feminists and all those seeking to replace outmoded paradigms and harmful social practices. Myths that erect roadblocks to reunions include the fear that adoptive parents will lose their children, that lives will be disrupted, and that reunitees and their families will be hurt by the meeting. Reunions represent risk-taking behaviour. But so does starting a new job, getting married, having a child and any of the other life-changing events we all experience. They also represent, like these other rites of passage, a huge potential for personal growth and hap-piness.

Research has pointed overwhelmingly to the positive potential of reunions. The majority of reunitees have no regrets about their meeting. Personal well-being, in both birth mothers and adoptees, is almost universally reported to be enhanced through a reunion. Likewise, relationships between adoptees and their adoptive parents improve, in most cases, when the adoptive parents are informed of the reunion.

Although the cliché of the adoptee having the door slammed in her face by her birth mother does occur, it is rare. As always, popular mythology capitalizes on the sensational rather than portraying the norm. Yet even these fantastic sto-ries have not thwarted the momentum of reunions. Huge wait-ing lists exist across the country for those looking for informa-tion about their counterparts, and reunion registries are swamped with backlogs too large to service efficiently.

While post-adoption reunions are a relatively new phenom-enon, they are becoming extremely popular. But it's clear that there is still a lot of work to be done in the area of adoption and post-adoption reunions. As data are gathered, much will be learned from the experiences of reunitees. There are impor-tant implications for many fields, among them social work, psychology, psychiatry and genetics research. Because of the courage of yesterday's adoption participants who are talking about their experiences of adoption and reunion, the path will be smoothed for more healthy, psychologically sound adop-tions in the future.

§

PART TWO

THE PROCESS
OF REUNION

CHAPTER 6

THE SEARCH

I was one of the lucky ones. I found my mother through a provincial registry. Within five months of sending in my application, I met her. It went so fast, yet it was something I'd wanted to do for 28 years. Sometimes it seemed as though those five months lasted an eternity.

— M. M.

SELDOM IS A MIND as feverish as one that is set on finding a relative who has not been seen since birth. Once the decision is made to search, most people become obsessed with their quest. Sometimes they lose perspective, neglecting family, job, friends and even their health. Support and understanding from the loved ones of an adoptee or birth mother are extremely important at this time. A support group of others going through the same experience is invaluable, as only they will recognize and fully understand the feelings and difficulties involved in the search.

Jackie, a 32-year-old adoptee who launched a search for her birth mother, says it was difficult for her husband to understand why she would want to "invade somebody's life." Jackie told her spouse, "You've got all your answers. You've got brothers and sisters who look like you." Now, Jackie observes, "My husband is slowly beginning to understand, but when the search was an obsession with me, he found it really difficult."

On the other hand, some adoptees whose efforts as teenagers to gain information about their birth family have failed may develop a passive attitude. It's amazing how patiently adult adoptees can accept two- to four-year waiting periods for even the most meagre background information about their birth families — information to which they're legally entitled. Because of childhood experiences that left them feeling that it *wasn't* acceptable to search or to ask for information about their birth families, most adoptees have waited years for the courage to do so. When they are told they must wait many additional months or years to receive information, these adoptees typically respond with resignation. Burying and denying their needs for information about their origins have by now become second nature.

However, once adoptees have some information about their birth families, many decide to search. And once the search has begun, many of these adoptees become obsessively single-minded. This happens because, for the first time in their lives, their birth family becomes "real" to them, and the desire to know all becomes overwhelming.

For the adoptee or birth mother who has no background information to use as clues in her search, this waiting period adds to the weeks, months or years her search will take. Some searchers spend ten years from the time they begin their search until they reach their goal. Not only is searching logistically time-consuming, it is emotionally draining, and most searchers have to take a break from time to time to recharge their emotional batteries. It's not a bad idea to pace yourself and to take it slowly, allowing time out whenever necessary.

There are at least five ways people generally go about

searching for a birth relative or an adoptee. Currently, the search methods most commonly followed are: (1) contacting provincial adoption disclosure registries; (2) conducting a search through a group of peers who meet for that purpose; (3) organizing your own search; (4) hiring a private search consultant; or (5) hiring a private detective.

Hiring private search consultants or private detectives is a costly way of searching and, in the case of the latter, it's a risky proposition. Private detectives seldom have as well-developed resources as most volunteer search organizations, and for that reason they usually take longer to complete the task, if at all.

Rosemary hired a private detective to search for her birth daughter when her daughter was 17 years old.

"I met the detective when he came to a Parent Finders meeting one night," remembers Rosemary. "He didn't tell us how he did his searches, but, basically, he was doing the same things we were. I thought that because he was an ex-cop, he would have a few more sources to fall back on.

"When I hired him, he wanted a hundred dollars up front and I said, you show me that you can do something, then I'll give you the money. He said he'd have my daughter's name and address in three days.

"The third day came, and there was no phone call. The fourth day came, then the fifth. I couldn't concentrate on my work; I was a basket case. Finally, I called him and he said, 'I'm really sorry but my sources didn't work out.' I said, 'Why in heaven's name didn't you call me? I've been going crazy.' Now he's skipped the country. He never got a cent out of me, but I was pretty discouraged."

Rosemary's anecdote highlights the danger inherent in hiring private detectives who don't specialize in adoption reunions. Even if they do find the relative you are seeking, they may not have the special qualifications needed to be sensitive to all your needs, particularly your emotional needs.

Looking for a birth relative is a highly charged emotional undertaking. You'll need all the sensitivity and understanding you can get, including personal attention and consideration. A private searcher who specializes in locating lost relatives, and who usually has a degree in social work or similar training, will probably be more sensitive to the very specific issues that will crop up during the search. For example, they'll understand the need for their client to be informed at frequent intervals of the progress they're making. They'll also understand the importance of not arousing false hopes in their client, and the potential for disappointment if a mistake is made.

Private search consultants are few and far between, and they may not have any advantages in terms of resources and knowledge compared to a private search organization. One benefit, though, is that they will focus the search for you, and they may therefore complete it in less time than you might be able to. The time savings, however, will be offset by higher fees.

Searching alone, like hiring a private detective, also puts you at risk. Because the search will dredge up fears, pain, hope and many other emotions, you'll find that searching in a vacuum is a very difficult, if not impossible, undertaking.

Volunteer search organizations are usually your best bet. Their fees are low, and they have the resources, expertise, networks and track record to allow you the most efficient and supportive search experience. You'll also get support from those who can truly empathize with your goals. After all, these volunteers share the same aspirations. (See Appendix C for contacts.)

Provincial registries are set up in most Canadian provinces. If there's an adoption disclosure registry in your province, get your name on it, as well as on the list at Parent Finders, the largest national volunteer search organization in Canada. Addresses and telephone numbers for the provincial registries may be found in Appendix B. While you're waiting for a response, join a local volunteer organization, roll up your sleeves and get started on your own search.

WHO'S SEARCHING?

It's mostly women who are involved in searches and reunions. While more men are gradually becoming involved, usually a man who has a reunion is a birth father or an adoptee who was searched for — by a woman. Some social workers have theories about why more women than men are involved, but no comprehensive studies have been concluded that might shed light on why this is so. The best, although somewhat superficial, rationale is that women tend to work harder at establishing relationships. The birth mother lived through the experience of the pregnancy, birth and, in the majority of cases, through the adoption as well. While the birth mother established a bond with her newborn through the birth process, the birth father frequently did not even see his child.

According to my own and others' research and observations, as well as statistics from provincial adoption disclosure registries, approximately 80 percent of all birth parents who are searching are birth mothers and 20 percent are birth fathers. More female birth siblings seem to search for a sibling who was given up for adoption, compared to male birth siblings. Similarly, female adoptees who request information about their birth families tend to outnumber male adoptees by approximately two to one. The ratio is even higher for birth parents, with birth mothers seeking information about a child in a ratio of three to one compared to birth fathers.

While male adoptees comprise approximately 50 percent of adoptees having reunions, this is probably because their birth mothers are looking for them, not because male adoptees themselves are searching. In fact, male adoptees are generally more reluctant than females to search for their birth mothers.

There may be several reasons for the lower numbers of men involved in reunions. With respect to birth fathers, many ended the relationship with the birth mother when they learned about the pregnancy. These men are usually not inclined to register in a provincial registry or to search for their offspring.

Legal barriers also impede a search for or by a birth father. For example, in Ontario, the staff of the provincial adoption disclosure registry are not allowed to search for a birth father merely because he was named by a birth mother. The birth father must be on record as having clearly indicated that he is the child's father. Even if a man steps forward claiming to be the adoptee's birth father, unless the records from the time of the adoption include a statement of paternity signed by him, or other conclusive evidence such as payments made by him during the pregnancy and/or after the birth to support the birth mother, he will not be allowed to register in a provincial registry or to request a search.

In observing the reactions of male adoptees when questioned about their apparent lack of interest in their birth mothers, I've discovered anger and pain at the root of their "disinterest." Male adoptees do not corner the market on anger towards their birth mothers. But while male adoptees' anger seems to prevent them from pursuing a search or from expressing interest in their background, female adoptees tend to search regardless of the anger they may feel.

Also, in male adoptees, there tends to be an underlying attitude of blame based on the double standard that the birth mother was a disreputable woman who deserved to be punished. This judgmental anger is seldom directed towards the birth father.

Sometimes men are intimidated by their own low numbers in the search process. One social worker, a past president of a large Parent Finders group, comments, "I get an equal number of calls from men and women, but it's most often the women who follow up and come to meetings. It's a vicious circle. If men do feel comfortable enough to come out to a meeting, they arrive and see that there are only three or four other men and 25 women. That tends to confirm for them that they really don't want to get into it."

She agrees that there is more hostility among men towards their birth mothers. Men tend to camouflage their feelings by saying they just want the background information. They'll say they don't want to search because, "If she didn't want me then, why would she want me now?" They seem to be more afraid of pursuing a reunion, observes this social worker.

I've heard similar comments from adult male adoptees when I've asked whether or not they were interested in searching. When I tried to explain to one 35-year-old male adoptee the probability of his birth mother's pain about the relinquishment, he snapped, "She should have thought of that then, shouldn't she?"

Craig, a 25-year-old adoptee, says, "I never thought of looking for my parents. I can't see the point of looking for them when they leave you in the first place."

No studies have been done to determine what makes a male adoptee begin to search. However, the male adoptees I've met, ranging in age from 19 to 43, have one thing in common: curiosity. They all state that they are curious about the woman who gave birth to them.

PREPARING FOR A SEARCH

Before an adoptee or a birth mother begins her search, there are many things to consider in order to prepare for where the search might lead.

It's important to try to imagine the many scenarios and

possible outcomes of a search. Reading about the outcomes of the reunions of others in the upcoming chapters will be good preparation for the possibilities that may lie ahead. In addition, the following considerations are important:

Examine your emotional state and maturity, and gauge how emotionally strong you feel before you begin your search. Do you have a support system of loving friends and/or family who will stick by you throughout the search? Your search could take years and could involve a small fortune. Costs including airfare to hunt through distant archives or to follow up on a lead; postage and photocopying fees; long distance telephone charges; payment for documents and advertisements in newspapers; and time consumed are all part of the expense of conducting a search. These costs may accrue over the course of years. Do you have the mental stamina and the financial resources to continue over the long haul, or will you be disappointed if you have to quit, even temporarily?

For adoptees, adolescence may or may not be the right time to begin a search. It's already a time of major changes. For some adoptees, knowing their birth family history at this time may be the key to their mental health, yet they may be unable to cope with the results of a reunion. Others, especially if they have their adoptive family's full support, may be able to work through the difficult and confusing issues surrounding reunions.

Working out your feelings towards your birth mother or your relinquished child as far ahead of the reunion as possible is a good idea. A therapist or a trusted friend may be able to help you talk about and explore your feelings. This will enable you to meet your counterpart honestly and openly, once you've found her or him.

An adoptee's birth mother may have forgotten substantial aspects of the birth and relinquishment experiences, or these experiences may be too painful for her to talk about. As an adoptee, you may not be welcomed by her at all, or, in the worst-case scenario, she may deny that you're her child. For the birth mother, your son or daughter may not be ready to meet you when you're ready. It's commonly believed that an adoptee is not ready for a reunion until she reaches adulthood. Can you wait until the adoptee is emotionally prepared to meet you, if ever?

You may have many hidden expectations of your counterpart's personality, values, economic situation, and so on, and feel let down by contradictory circumstances. It's important to examine any expectations and prejudices you may have prior to a reunion. You may find someone of a different religion or, for the adoptee, of a different race or ethnic background from what you expect.

You must also prepare yourself to accept the fact that the person you seek may be deceased, which could be the unfortunate outcome of your search.

Most adoptees have half and/or full siblings who were born either before or after them. Remember, it's likely that once you meet one birth relative, many more may follow. Are you ready to suddenly welcome many more people into your life?[21]

PROVINCIAL REGISTRIES

Thousands of adoptees and birth mothers are successful in their searches every year. Many of them find each other through provincial adoption disclosure registries. Many registries vary in the services they offer, but, typically, they are government offices that keep registrations received from adoptees, birth parents and, in some provinces, birth siblings and birth grandparents, who wish to have a reunion with an adoptee. Typically, registrations are kept on file indefinitely, and are only removed at the written request of the registrant.

By the end of 1992, nearly 12,000 names were on Ontario's provincial adoption disclosure registry. For this reason, and because of the lack of funding for the program and a subsequent shortage of staff at that time, it took approximately one year for a new registration to be processed. Other provinces are a little faster because of fewer registrations due to lower populations. Registries that match only incoming registrants with each other are called "passive" registries. Provincial registries that will actively search for a birth parent or an adoptee are called "active" registries.

In the case of provincial registries that conduct searches in which there is no "match" between an adoptee and a birth relative, the demand for this service is great and the staff is minimal. A search may take several months once it has begun, but if there are thousands of names before yours, you might wait several years for your turn. If the registry cannot locate you at the time they are ready to begin your search, they will skip over your name and go on to the next person. So it's important to keep your address and telephone number up-to-date in provincial registries.

Newfoundland, Nova Scotia, New Brunswick, Ontario, Manitoba, Saskatchewan, Alberta and British Columbia have central adoption registries. There is also a passive registry in the Yukon. In Quebec, P.E.I. and the Northwest Territories, there is no central registry. An adoptee or birth family member should contact the provincial office listed in Appendix B or the agency where the adoption took place for services. Some provinces, such as Ontario, have registries whose practices are defined by legislation, while other provinces establish their own policies. If no legislation exists giving specified parties a legal right to service, registry clients must depend solely on the judgment of the provincial staff, who determine whether or not they will conduct a search in any particular case. Appendices B and C list national and provincial post-adoption registries and search groups currently in existence.

While provincial registries overlap in some areas of service, the specific laws or regulations governing their procedures vary widely. In most provinces, registration is free, while in others a fee is charged to register, to receive non-identifying information and/or to have a search conducted on your behalf. In some provinces, pre-reunion counselling is mandatory by law. In other provinces, such as British Columbia, clients are simply given each other's addresses and telephone numbers and left to take it from there. No counselling is provided.

Searches for birth relatives on behalf of adult adoptees are done in the Northwest Territories and in all provinces except Alberta and the Yukon. In Quebec and P.E.I. a search may be undertaken on request, but not through a provincial adoption registry. As of October 1991, birth parents may also request a search in British Columbia, which, as of that date, was the only province where birth parents could search through a provincial registry. However, a search through this registry costs $250. All other provinces except Saskatchewan offered their services free of charge as of 1991.

The lack of consistency and co-ordination among Canadian provinces is typical of North American adoption and post-adoption practice. Adoptees and birth mothers having to cross the border will find that in the United States, legislation and practice also vary widely from state to state, ranging from anti-quated, restrictive laws to open-record policies.

The inconsistencies among provinces causes problems on many levels. First of all, the flow of information is impeded due to the lack of a well-established information network. It is rare to find a social worker in one province who knows what's going on in another province, let alone in another city. This makes it difficult to service clients who were adopted out-of-province. Expertise is sorely lacking in many areas due to this information "blackout."

The inequity of one person having to pay for a service while another receives it free of charge is an obvious flaw, and injustices also arise when, in one province, the elderly are given precedence while in another, they're put on a waiting list along with everyone else. It's no wonder that many adoptees and birth parents feel discouraged as they race against time to find an aging counterpart. Their search may well end in disappointment.

PUBLIC AGENCIES

To obtain information for their searches, adult adoptees, adoptive parents, birth parents and, in some provinces, adult birth relatives may request non-identifying information from the public agency that handled an adoption. Non-identifying information is background history about the birth parents or about the adoptive family and the adoptee. The information given to adoptees might include details such as the birth parents' ethnic background, a description of the physical and personality traits of birth family members, their level of academic achievement, occupational history, medical history and reasons for the adoption cited by the birth mother. No identifying details about the birth family are provided.

The birth mother or birth sibling requesting information will receive details of the adoptee's infancy and development, up until the time the adoption was legally finalized, and general information about the adoptive parents, including their ages, physical descriptions, occupations, interests and whether or not there were other children in the family at the time of the adoption. Frequently, receipt of this information precedes the actual search or reunion and is used as the basis upon which the search proceeds.

The non-identifying information prepares the adoptee for the kind of person she might meet at her reunion. The information, unfortunately, can also be misleading. Debbie, an adoptee who met her birth sister through a social service agency, comments, "Half of the background information I received was a lie. My birth mother lied about who my birth father was."

Debbie's birth mother was not the only one to change or omit facts. Yesterday's birth mothers sometimes falsified information to make their infant more "adoptable" in the competition for the "best" adoptive homes. It was not uncommon for the birth mother or birth grandparents to falsify the birth father's occupation. A doctor's child might be more readily adopted than a farm labourer's.[22]

Unfortunately, these inaccuracies have led more than one adoptee down a cold trail in pursuit of a birth parent. What you may have been told about your birth family or about an adoptee may not necessarily be the case. My own non-identifying information, which I received after my reunion, contained a number of erroneous "facts." Birth grandparents whom I'd already met were stated as being deceased, occupations were inaccurate, and so on. It was only after I'd met my birth family that I realized that this information was skewed.

VOLUNTEER SEARCH ORGANIZATIONS

Parent Finders is the most commonly known volunteer search organization and it is well-established across Canada.

Jackie, an adoptee, first connected with other adoptees at a Parent Finders meeting. "For people who are beginning a search," she advises, "there is always someone there who is also beginning. If you are nearing the end of a search, there is somebody there who's been through it or who is also getting close to having a reunion. You can sit down with that person and have a gab session or a gripe session. You both understand what the other person is feeling, better than anyone in your family, because no one in your family has gone through it."

Joan Vanstone of Vancouver established the first Parent Finders organization in 1974 to assist adult adoptees in Canada. Today, the organization has spread to almost every major city across Canada. A national, computerized registry is maintained in Vancouver, British Columbia.

Mary Beth Hoy is a social worker and past president of the London, Ontario, chapter of Parent Finders. The London group is split evenly between adoptees and birth parents, says Hoy, but some birth grandparents have also joined. Some adoptees bring along their adoptive parent or parents, usually their adoptive mother, for support.

Birth mother Rosemary remembers being coaxed to attend her first Parent Finders meeting. "There were lots of birth mothers there," says Rosemary. "I walked into the room and heard people talking about adoption and I fled. I couldn't stand these people talking about it. But somebody came running after me. They brought me back and I sat through the whole meeting and bawled, because I heard everyone else expressing their experiences, which were so like mine. That was a really draining night. I walked away feeling so much better. I felt like a human being again, that I was just one out of millions who were experiencing the same thing. I wasn't alone anymore.

"Finally, after about the eighth or ninth meeting, I wasn't crying anymore and I was actually talking to other people. I ended up, eventually, helping new members come in. I would say to them, 'I know how you're feeling,' and they'd say, 'No, you don't,' and I'd answer, 'Oh yes, I do,' and we'd both sit there and have a good cry."

While the group is called *Parent Finders*, birth parents are also beginning to search in greater numbers. One group for both parties is helpful, because adoptees and birth mothers can give each other insights into the other's experiences and help prepare each other for the road ahead. They can also support each other in their disappointments and triumphs. On a practical level, they can share resources since the mechanics of their searches are similar, if not identical.

Membership fees, set by each group, range from 25 dollars to 60 dollars. The fee covers operating costs and registration in the national registry in Vancouver. For an extra five to ten dollars, you can receive the national monthly Parent Finders newsletter.

Not all members are there to search. "Some people come for support," says Hoy, "and that's especially true of older people in their sixties and seventies, who grew up in a time when adoption wasn't even talked about, when it was a deep, dark secret. They come out to share their feelings and to talk to people they feel will understand."

The ages of group members range from 18 to 71, but the average age of the London group is 34, which is typical of other Parent Finders groups, says Hoy. Calls from younger adoptees and birth parents who have relinquished children who are not yet 18 are met with a cautious response. This reflects the belief that adoptees under the age of 18 or 19 are not emotionally prepared to have a reunion and that it's better to wait until they are older for the birth parent to begin her search.

Jackie's frustration with her difficult search for her birth mother was partly alleviated by her participation in Parent Finders. "I was so glad there was a support group, so I could go in and blow off a little steam. There was somebody else there who had been searching for seven years, and she could understand what I was feeling," recalls Jackie.

Experienced group members will offer to make the first telephone contact with a newly located birth relative or adoptee. Members are encouraged to exercise discretion and tact when making these initial contacts, which is part of the code of ethics penned at the inception of Parent Finders. The organization sometimes acts as a political lobbying group as well.

"We're a group that's becoming more known and more verbal in what we want. We're trying to fight restrictive legislation and to get financial assistance from the government," explains Jackie. "But we're not being acknowledged fast enough. The provincial government doesn't know the mental and emotional anguish that somebody goes through in a search, and you can't explain it to somebody who hasn't been through it."

When the Canadian Adoption Reunion Register Search and Support Group (CARR) was formed in May 1987, an advertisement was placed in a Toronto newspaper inviting those involved with adoption to attend a meeting. After the first large turnout, says Pat Richardson, one of the founders of CARR and an adoptee herself, "We really dwindled, because we didn't advertise."

CARR has refrained from stating a specific mandate, hoping that people who have searched successfully will be on hand to help new members joining the group. Richardson says CARR strives to focus on "a lot of warmth, a lot of feeling, and a lot of help." While at present CARR is avoiding a political thrust and a hierarchical structure, its goals may well change as the group evolves.

Richardson instructs adoptees to write down everything they've been told or imagine they were told about their adoption, before attending their first meeting. She advises them to try to find their Adoption Order, the court document that legally finalized their adoption. Experienced members of CARR then help new members glean useful information from these papers and memories. New members are also told about the central adoption disclosure registry in Toronto, how to register, and how to obtain their background information. But, says Richardson, "We tell them that it's going to take a long time through the registry and that they will find their families faster through us." Since provincial funding for post-adoption services is continually being cut back, this is becoming even more the case.

Just as in Parent Finders, members of CARR are encouraged to conduct their own searches. Richardson maintains, "Part of our mental health is that we do our own searches. We gain a lot of strength and a lot of power from doing that."

Meetings begin with a brief recounting by one of the members of a personal reunion story or a relevant aspect of adoption search and reunion. Then members break into search groups, "so we can get down to what we came here for," says Richardson.

SEARCH ETHICS

If a provincial registry is handling your search, you won't have to consider the ethics of the search, because the parameters of your search will already be in place. Most Parent Finders groups also have clearly defined search ethics. But if you are conducting your own search, you should take the following into consideration.

If you're an adoptee searching for your birth mother, keep in mind that she may have married after your birth. Her husband and subsequent children may be unaware of your existence. Similarly, extended birth family relatives may or may not know about you. Birth mothers should remember that while most adoptees know they were adopted, some may not. In each of these cases, the utmost tact and care must be exercised in gleaning the particulars of the situation, before proceeding with caution.

While the searcher has had weeks, months or years to prepare mentally for the search and its outcome, the person sought will most likely be thrown completely off guard. Remember there are two distinct roles here, and it may take time for the found person to adjust to having been "found."

Honesty is always important. In a search, the end does not necessarily justify the means. How would you feel if you resorted to deceitful or unethical measures to find your counterpart?

How would they feel if they found out? It's better to explore all possible routes before employing less-than-ethical methods, such as lying about your identity, looking at documents that are private or asking someone else to do either of these for you.

SEARCH HINTS

This book is not intended to replace search groups or search experts. However, here's a sampling of the kinds of tools other searchers have used successfully in the past.

Many adoptees can find their original birth name on their Adoption Order, the court-issued document that finalizes an adoption. The Adoption Order is worth its weight in gold if it has your birth name on it. Some adoptive parents have a copy of the Order. If you feel comfortable doing so, ask your adoptive parents if you can see your Adoption Order or a copy of it. The Order will also tell you which court finalized the adoption, which provides a clue to your birth mother's whereabouts at the time of your adoption.

Birthparents should remember that the names of adoptees who were adopted as infants have been legally changed to their adoptive parents' surnames. Usually, their given names are also changed. But sometimes the adoptive parents will retain one given birth name. They may also name their child after themselves or an adoptive relative.

Similarly, adoptees should know that in most cases, their birth mother was unmarried at the time of their adoption. Therefore, most adoptees have their birth mother's maiden name as their original surname, *not* their birth father's surname. Also, your original birth names may provide clues to other birth family members' names. Frequently, birth mothers have named their son after the birth father, or their daughter after a sister, mother or aunt.

All paperwork associated with the adoption, including the Adoption Order, correspondence, medical forms, and so on, can yield valuable clues to help you in your search. Try to get your hands on as much documentation as possible.

City directories and business directories are the ultimate search tools; they can be found in public libraries or in university libraries. Occupations, names of businesses, number of occupants in a household, street addresses, telephone numbers and names are all listed and organized in several ways. Most searchers use city and business directories at some point, applying the information they already have at their disposal to the directory. For example, if a birth mother knows there were two other children in the adoptive home before the adoption, she knows there were three at the time of the adoption. If she's also told that the adoptive father was a professional, she can put these two pieces of information together to find, say, doctor so-and-so in such-and-such a city, probably the city where she relinquished her child. If she can verify that this doctor has three children, voilà! She's begun to narrow down the possibilities.

After I'd met my birth mother and her family, I found myself wanting to meet my birth father also. On the advice of a friend who was a birth mother, I paid a small sum to the Ministry of Transportation and Communications and requested a Driver Record Search. For a mere five dollars, I was able to fill out an application form, providing my birth father's name and year of birth, and every licensed Ontario driver's record was searched. Two weeks later, I got a negative response in the mail. They hadn't found anyone with that name and birth date.

I tried again, using the previous year, and this time the computer generated my birth father's name and address, which were mailed to me. After a telephone call to Bell Canada, I had his phone number. Telephone directories for cities across Canada are available in public libraries. Once I had his telephone number, all I had to do was summon the courage to call.

Another resource is your local newspaper. It's impossible to pick up a newspaper today and not find several advertisements run by birth mothers or adoptees who are searching for each other. Typically run on the adoptee's birthday, ads usually include the adoptee's birth name and date of birth, the hospital where she was born, and a Post Office box number. If you plan to run an ad, make sure you're ready for a response. The results can be head-spinningly sudden; or it could take weeks, months or years for a reluctant adoptee or birth mother to finally respond. For this reason, it's wise to advertise a permanent box number, such as one that's set up by a search organization specifically for that purpose.

WHAT IT FEELS LIKE TO SEARCH

After regularly attending Parent Finders meetings, Rosemary one day found the courage to place an advertisement in several newspapers in cities where she felt her birth daughter might live. On her daughter's 18th birthday, she ran the ad.

Rosemary got a phone call two months later from her friend Jan, another member of Parent Finders. Jan had picked up an envelope for Rosemary at the Parent Finders' Post Office box; it was addressed simply to "Rosemary." "I slammed the phone down and hopped in my car," Rosemary recalls.

"Normally, it's a ten-minute drive, but I think I made it to Jan's in five-and-a-half minutes. I opened the envelope. I was shaking and had tears coming down my eyes so thickly I couldn't read. I said, 'Jan, you're going to have to read it.' She read it and started to cry, too."

When you do your own search, one of the risks is finding the wrong person. Rosemary worried about this.

Joanne, Rosemary's daughter, was wondering the same thing. Joanne asked Rosemary to write to her to confirm that she was really her birth mother.

Rosemary began her letter that night. "The waste basket was full. By six o'clock in the morning, I finally had the letter together," says Rosemary. "I hadn't eaten. I hadn't slept. My hair was a mess. I still had the same clothes on from the day before. I hadn't even been to bed. I thought, I'm not going to get keyed up. But in the meantime, I was just about splitting my sides, I was so excited."

Because Rosemary had been briefed by Parent Finders, she knew to ask Joanne if she had access to her non-identifying information, and if so, she knew she could use this information to help prove whether or not she'd found her daughter. If Joanne's information described Rosemary, the birth families and the circumstances accurately, Rosemary knew the chances were good that she'd found her birth daughter.

Joanne read her non-identifying information to Rosemary over the telephone.

"It said I worked in a hospital, and it described my sister's family. I said, 'Joanne, you've got the right person.'"

Ursula, who had also joined a Parent Finders group, decided to search for her birth son, Stephen. Ursula had been told by the agency where she had placed Stephen that he had been adopted by a Hungarian family. She ran an advertisement in a newspaper and received an unsigned letter.

Ursula comments, "I wanted to make sure that I didn't have someone playing a game with me. I had to have more proof. I checked out the return address in the city directory right away. The name was French, so I thought, 'Oh my God, he was adopted by a French family, this isn't right.'" Ursula later learned that this man was indeed her son, but that he had used a friend's return address, not his own, on the envelope.

Many searchers find a birth relative other than their birth mother first, and they then use information about and from that relative to help them locate their birth mother.

Laura, an adoptee, located a woman she believed to be her birth aunt, and travelled across four provinces to verify her information. When she arrived at her destination, Laura telephoned her aunt, who was then 75 years old, and told her she was doing research on the Campbell family. Laura was invited to her birth aunt's home that afternoon.

Laura recalls, "I hung up the phone and thought, I have to get my hair right, my makeup right. I had to choose the most professional-looking thing I could wear, because not only was I portraying someone who was doing research, but I also might be revealing who I really was. This would be the first impression and it was important because that impression was going to go to my birth mother."

When Laura arrived at the woman's home, she was settled in a comfortable chair. Then, remembers Laura, "My aunt told me all these stories about the family. I just sat there and took notes. I wrote down stories about my grandfather and his two older brothers, which brother drowned and what my great-grandfather did for a living. She started showing me photographs, but still didn't give me any indication that she thought something fishy was going on. Meanwhile, three hours went by."

Laura says, "By this time, I had what I wanted. I knew where my birth mother was. I could have walked away. But instead, I told my aunt I had something that I wanted to share with her before she went any further. She was being honest with me. I wanted to be honest with her."

Laura decided to share her non-identifying information with her aunt. Laura's aunt read the information and, although she remarked on similarities between her family and what she was reading, she still didn't seem to realize that it was her own family she was reading about.

"Finally, she came to the part about 'putative father,' and she asked me what that meant. At this point, I was shaking. I said 'putative father' meant my birth father, my blood father. She looked at me, and my eyes were very teary. I said, fill in all the blanks with 'Mary,' which was my birth mother's name, her sister. She said, 'Oh my god.' I said, 'Yes, I'm adopted. That's why I'm here."

Laura's aunt was happy to learn of Laura's true identity. "She hugged me and said, 'If you only knew all the times that I've thought about you.' She said she'd wondered about who had adopted me, was I happy, had I been taken care of. She also said that if she had known about the pregnancy earlier, she would have asked to adopt me."

Laura had been searching for ten years. Her tenacity paid off. Although searchers often feel like giving up, the rewards are great for those who persevere — and every searcher ends up with more information than when they started. Because of its many demands, a search can help to build the stamina it will take to endure the outcome of a reunion, whatever that may be.

THINGS TO REMEMBER

Given the difficulties of a search, these guidelines may help keep you alert to both your own needs and the sought-after person's needs:

FOR THE ADOPTEE:

(1) Searching is your birthright.
(2) You know you're adopted; your birth mother's family might not. Tread carefully.

FOR THE BIRTH MOTHER:

(1) You have a right to follow up on the well-being of your birth child, but not to be part of their adult life unless you are invited to participate.

(2) Most adoptees are not ready to meet their birth mothers until their mid- to late twenties.
(3) You know your son or daughter was adopted; they might not know.

FOR THE ADOPTIVE PARENTS:

(1) The adult adoptee is not looking to replace you. If the adoptee is an adult, you have already done the parenting.
(2) A search does not mean you've failed as parents.

FOR ALL:

(1) Make sure you're mentally, emotionally and financially ready before you search. A search and reunion changes the searcher's life and the lives of those around her, forever.
(2) Have a support system in place before searching, whether it's your family, a search group, a therapist and/or a devoted friend. Find someone who will listen without being judgmental.
(3) It's okay to be focussed; it's harmful to be too obsessed. Strive for balance.

§

CHAPTER 7

BACKSTAGE:
PRE-REUNION JITTERS

*I needed the support of a counsellor before my reunion, espe-
cially the day before, when I really panicked. But after I first
learned that my birth mother had also registered, I needed
lots of time alone to come to grips with what was about to
happen: I was going to meet my birth mother. It took a while
for this to sink in. I felt like I had a great secret and couldn't
share it with anyone.*

— M. M.

WHETHER YOU'VE SEARCHED for years to find your birth family, or, as in my case, registered in a provincial adoption disclosure registry and had a "match" with a birth family member
who also registered, once the reunion looms on the horizon,
your life is thrown into turmoil.

Having a reunion is like throwing your emotions into a
blender at high speed. Elation, despair, panic, fear, all mix
together, churning in the pit of your stomach. Your thoughts
whirl and you can't concentrate; you may think you're going
crazy. Or maybe you're unnaturally calm, numbed by the

overwhelming bombardment of so many feelings at once. Perhaps you're scared to death and unwilling to allow yourself to feel anything at all.

There are numerous and far-ranging issues that face reunitees as they move towards and through their reunion. Some reunion issues are similar for both the birth mother and the adoptee; others are role-specific.

For those who wish to develop a relationship after the reunion, it is especially important to move slowly and to entertain as few expectations as possible. When difficulties arise, they are frequently the result of disparities between the adoptee's wishes and dreams for the future, and those of her birth mother.

"There are differences in the definition of success from searcher to searcher," says Mary Beth Hoy, who, as a past president of Parent Finders, has witnessed many reunions. "An adoptee might say, for example, 'If I meet my birth mother, and don't get the door slammed in my face, that's all I want — just to ask some questions, to get some information.' But if that adoptee's birth mother thinks, 'Here's my little girl!' and is hoping for a relationship, there may be problems."

The trick to successful reunion is to focus on its positive aspects, regardless of whether you meet once or develop an ongoing relationship.

THE ADOPTEE'S EXPERIENCE

It's natural to feel ambivalence and anxiety when facing the unknown. As a reunion approaches, adoptees, like birth parents, experience fears and apprehension at this turning point in their lives.

Shortly after I received the notice that my birth mother had registered, I began to feel guilty about having registered at all. It was only a year after my adoptive mother's death and here I was, about to meet my birth mother. Was I trying to replace the mother I had lost through death?

My decision to apply to the Adoption Disclosure Registry seemed inevitable. It just happened, a part of a natural process that couldn't be stopped. My adoptive father felt the same way, and signed his consent for my application with the remark, "I wondered when you'd get around to doing this." He was as excited as I when he heard the news of my upcoming reunion. Together, we anticipated meeting the woman who had given me life.

Even though I understood the reasons for my adoption, childhood feelings of abandonment welled up, choking me with pain. My reunion was sickening, yet at the same time integral to my health. I knew I had to go through with this to overcome the emptiness I had felt all my life.

MANDATORY COUNSELLING

Before I met my birth mother, I attended mandatory counselling with a social worker. In Ontario, these sessions are legislated and are thus unavoidable for anyone who has registered with the provincial adoption registry. When I learned of this legal imposition, I was outraged. If requiring permission from your adoptive parents to register wasn't bad enough, now I couldn't help but feel patronized by being forced into "counselling." For what? Reunion wasn't a problem — it was a solution.

Confident from the start, I believed I had dealt with all the issues long ago. Hadn't I been considering the repercussions of a reunion for 28 years? Full of indignation, I attended my first counselling session.

I was well-educated, intelligent, sensitive. What could they tell me that I hadn't already figured out? Plenty. Through my social worker, Cathy, I realized that reunions with birth parents weren't like meeting a new neighbour or a distant cousin. A reunion was like a suddenly exploding bomb: the fallout could be painful and unpredictable.

I began to realize that I had expected to meet the mother of my childhood dreams. I held preconceived notions of who my birth mother was, some of which turned out to be hauntingly correct. But other preconceptions proved to be wildly out of step. Many were, in fact, ideals that no human mother could ever meet.

Gord, an adoptee, comments, "I had convinced myself that I wasn't expecting anything. Whoever she is, that's great. I'll accept that. Then when I started talking to Sharon [Gord's social worker], I realized that I was expecting something after all. I had been envisioning family get-togethers with all these people I didn't know [birth relatives], seeing my birth mother on a regular basis, and feeling this real bond when I met her. Sharon put things into a more realistic perspective."

My social worker asked if I had considered the possibility that my birth family of German origin might have cultural values that clashed with my adopted, middle-class, Scottish heritage. I hadn't. She asked whether I could accept my birth mother if she was radically different from the people in my adoptive family. What if she were rich? Or poor? I simply wasn't sure.

Gord vividly recalls his pre-reunion feelings. "You analyse yourself totally," he says, "I had just turned 19 and I thought, great, I'm 19 years old and I've got braces. She's going to think I'm a doorknob.

"I'd only finished a year of college, and I had just landed a job at Sears. I thought my mother would think I was stupid, and wonder why I wasn't in university. I was afraid I wasn't going to be who she wanted me to be."

Like Gord, I too felt a heightened insecurity before my reunion. I worried not only about how I would look, but also about what I would say, how I would act — everything. Despite my initial rebelliousness, my social worker helped a lot by reassuring me that my insecurities were very common, and were very likely shared by my birth mother.

In the pre-reunion process, adoptees and birth mothers who meet through an adoption disclosure registry are often given background or non-identifying information about their counterpart. Sometimes there is also an exchange of letters and photographs before the actual meeting. My social worker took notes as I dictated the details of my life: my occupation, the colour of my eyes and hair, what kind of music I liked. Later, she read aloud bits and pieces of my birth mother's life to me.

Next, I wrote my birth mother a letter that would be forwarded to her through our respective social workers. I wondered how I could tell her about myself without revealing too much or too little. I finally attempted the impossible: painting a picture she'd love, without knowing if her tastes were Cézanne or Warhol.

When my birth mother's first letter arrived, handwritten and addressed to "Diana," my birth name, I called Cathy, my social worker, in horror. This woman had poured her heart and soul into these pages, while my letter now seemed stilted and cold by comparison. I'd actually typed my letter because I was afraid my handwriting would repel her! Cathy calmed me and suggested I write again, expressing my fears. I did so, and felt that an equal exchange had been initiated.

When my birth mother's letters arrived, friends and family concurred: "She sounds so much like you!" After 28 years of separation, I found the similarity in our personalities and viewpoints uncanny, creating a weird mixture of shock and comfort before my reunion.

I wrote in my journal after receiving my birth mother's second letter: "How could I have possibly gained all these things from you — the love of poetry, art, music? Is there a gene to carry all this, a memory in my brain that somehow absorbed your personality? I am so confused, bewildered and delighted." Again, Cathy was instrumental in explaining to me that what I was experiencing was actually quite common among adoptees and that many share similarities in aptitudes, mannerisms, tastes and values with their birth families.

As we've seen, before a reunion, birth mothers often suffer pangs of guilt about their decision to relinquish their child. Fear of their child's anger may slow down the pace of a reunion. Ironically, most adoptees say that they do not feel anger prior to the meeting, but that they simply want to gain information and to meet someone who looks like them, and then they want to race, unbridled, towards the reunion.

My social worker was the only person who could have curtailed my wild impulse to run blindly into my birth mother's arms, regardless of the consequences. Gord, whose reunion was also the result of a match in a provincial registry, felt as I did. "As soon as I knew there was a match," says Gord, "I wanted to meet her, that day. I know now that counselling is important, but when you're going through it, you think, 'Let's get it over with, just let me meet her.'"

Rushing into a reunion is never a good idea. "Even though people say to me, over and over again, 'I'm prepared for whatever happens,'" says social worker Mary Beth Hoy, "they're actually not prepared. You think you know how you're going to feel, but you really don't." Social workers strongly recommend that if you are not willing to accept all imaginable background circumstances, you are not yet ready for a reunion.

While I had the benefit of counselling and the advantage of exchanging letters with my birth mother before our meeting, the situation is different for adoptees who have conducted their own search and for whom counselling is not mandatory. Counselling is an important aspect of preparing for a reunion. A person searching privately requires just as much professional support. The difficulty is that it's rare to find a therapist who has experience in this field. Occasionally, though, social workers who counsel reunitees who have been matched through a provincial registry will also counsel people who have done their own search.

SUPPORT FROM OTHERS

There are several potential sources of support, other than a counsellor, for the adoptee who is about to have a reunion.

If an adoptee has told his or her adoptive parents of the search and the upcoming reunion, they might prove to be a good source of support. Gord's adoptive mother offered to drive him to his reunion, and once they arrived, she offered to go in with him.

Adoptive parents who, as we've seen, have their own fears about the reunion, can also intensify the adoptee's anxiety.

Gord says, "I remember the day before my reunion. No one was talking about it at my house. My mom was very threatened, not that she said so. But I knew her well enough to know that. I remember lying awake, smoking cigarettes and drinking ice water and knowing that if I went upstairs and said, 'I don't want to do this,' my parents would say, 'Thank God!' And the relief would be wonderful for everybody. It was like I was holding the torch by myself. They didn't mean to hurt me. They just didn't understand."

When the adoptive parents are not supportive, adoptees can feel isolated while awaiting the reunion. This feeling is exacerbated when friends are also uncomfortable, unsupportive or outright opposed to the upcoming meeting.

The night before his reunion, Gord went to a friend's party. "I was sitting on the patio by a pool with some friends, and I almost fell off my chair. I said, 'Do you guys realize what I'm doing tomorrow?' It was like it hit me in the face at that moment. Nobody else understood."

Sean found his birth mother and is searching for his birth father. He says, "People who know I'm adopted don't know that I'm looking. I've had the same friend for 22 years. We met when we were in baby carriages. He was the best man at my wedding and even he doesn't know. He's my best friend, but that's not something I would talk to him about."

One of the reasons adoptees may not share their story is fear of disapproval. They find it frustrating and difficult to face accusations from those who don't understand or agree with their desire for a reunion, particularly from those who haven't been adopted.

Gord says, "I had a close friend who was totally against it [the reunion]. He said, 'I can't believe you're doing this. Your parents are your parents, how can you do this to them?'

"People would say to me, 'I can understand why you'd want to do that, because of health reasons.' And I'd say 'No! I don't care about health reasons. I'm just nosey. I want to know who gave birth to me. I just want to meet her.' I remember lying awake nights wanting to know who she was."

The strongest understanding and support can come from other adoptees who have had the same experiences. Before my own reunion, I compared notes with Vince, an adoptee who had met his birth mother three years previously. Vince and I had met at a public meeting on adoption reunions. The best thing I did to prepare for my reunion was to talk to Vince. When I spoke with him, he told me all the things he'd felt before his reunion, and his feelings mirrored mine exactly. Finally, I'd found someone who truly understood.

ADOPTEES IN LIMBO

Laura is in limbo.

"I wanted to search for my birth mother for half my life," says Laura, at age 40. Instead of finding her birth mother,

Laura found a birth aunt after three years of searching. Laura's aunt gave Laura her birth mother's address in December 1987. Six months later, Laura spoke with her birth mother for the first and only time.

After the years of yearning and the cost of searching (about $10,000, including her trip to the west coast to meet her birth aunt), Laura has a "love-hate" relationship with Mary, her birth mother.

Laura faithfully sends Christmas, birthday and Mother's Day cards to Mary, but has received neither phone calls nor correspondence in reply. One complicating factor is that Laura's birth mother had not told her husband — whom she met and married several years after Laura's adoption — about Laura's existence.

As time goes on, Laura says it's difficult for her not to feel it's her fault that her birth mother hasn't responded. "Maybe she thinks I'm a brat and wonders why she should have anything to do with me," worries Laura.

Laura's feelings are representative of those that mar an adoptee's childhood: guilt, rejection and helplessness. These feelings persist into adulthood and are intensified by the search. Especially, as in Laura's case, when the birth mother does not welcome the adoptee wholeheartedly into her life.

"I hate her for what she's done to me," says Laura. "And yet Mary could pick up that phone tomorrow and ask me to meet her anywhere and I would. That would wipe out any animosity I feel."

Jackie is another adoptee who is experiencing frustration, anger and bitterness at having found, but not having met, her birth mother.

Jackie was 28 years old when she learned her birth mother's address. Jackie wrote to ask this woman for confirmation that she was, indeed, her birth mother.

"I ran to the mailbox every day," says Jackie. "I couldn't

stand it any longer, so two months later, I called her. I wrote everything down on paper, her number, what I was going to say, and I stood there with my finger in the dial. It took me 20 minutes to finally dial the number."

After Jackie had identified herself, silence followed. Jackie forged ahead, asking the woman on the other end of the line if she had received her letter. The woman said she had read Jackie's letter, but didn't know how she could help.

"I was still questioning whether I had the right lady," says Jackie, "so I said, 'Can you tell me whether or not you are my birth mother?' Again there was silence and I thought, 'Lady, you don't know how hard this is for me.' She finally said, 'Yes.'"

Jackie spoke with her birth mother for 20 minutes. "I was determined not to hang up until I had her permission to phone again. After a few pokes and prods, she finally agreed." By the end of the call, Jackie was sobbing.

Like Laura, Jackie began to send her birth mother letters and cards, telling her about her life and her family, but receiving nothing in return. In her letters, Jackie assured her birth mother that she wasn't going to intrude and that she only wanted to begin a friendship and to give their relationship time.

A month later, Jackie called her birth mother again. "I tried to sound jovial," says Jackie, "as though there was nothing bothering me. But there was total silence. I asked her if it was a bad time for her to talk, and she said 'No, I can talk. But I have nothing to say.' I just gasped and said, 'Okay, goodbye.' That was it. I hung up. The third call ended the same way."

Jackie, like Laura, has driven past her birth mother's house in a desperate bid to glean more information. "I fantasized about impersonating a Fuller Brush lady," says Jackie, "and going to her door. But I'd already sent her my picture, so I couldn't do that for fear she'd slam the door in my face."

In another attempt to extract information, Jackie wrote to her birth mother before undergoing minor surgery.

"My doctor had asked for my medical history. I didn't tell my birth mother what the surgery was for, and I thought, 'Well, let's see if I can get some information out of you this way,' so I wrote to her. She wrote back listing all of her 25 allergies.

"When the rest of my letters went unanswered, it slowly started sinking in that I wasn't going to be a part of her life. I had to quit playing this foolish game of hope, of fantasy land. But it hurts. It hurts a lot," sighs Jackie.

"I'm angry that she never wrote back. She never acknowledged that I'm a person, that I am part of her, except that one confirmation on the phone. I start to wonder if she really is my birth mother. I start to wonder why she said 'yes' in the first place. By this point, I'm really angry and I'm getting bitter. I am a person and I deserve to be acknowledged."

Jackie has tried to put herself in her birth mother's place in order to cope with the situation. "I imagine she's contented with her life, but I would have to say that she does feel guilty. She's got to get over that."

When Jackie asked about her birth father, her birth mother began to cry and refused to discuss him. Jackie avoided the subject for a while, until her last letter to her birth mother. Jackie informed her birth mother that she was about to begin searching for her birth father.

Jackie displays a strength of character and a determination characteristic of others who experience the agony of searching. "I don't feel rejected," she states. "My mother doesn't know me, so she can't reject me. Not being accepted, or her inability to accept the situation as it is, that's a better way of putting it."

Nevertheless Jackie's frustration is apparent. "She had a Caesarean birth with me," Jackie explains. "I think, 'Every night when you get into your pajamas, or you have a bath, or you're changing, you see that scar. Am I just a scar in your life?' I don't want to be that."

Although her search has been painful, Jackie says she's learned a lot from the experience, including patience, determination and how to support others.

Both of Jackie's children are aware of Jackie's birth mother and know, vaguely, who she is. "My son, Andrew, will look at me and see the hurt I'm feeling," says Jackie, "and he'll put his arm around me and say, 'It's okay, mommy, I love you.' Or if I'm writing a letter to my birth mother, he'd like to sign his name or draw a picture in it.

"My adoptive mom is also very supportive," continues Jackie, whose adoptive father died three years before she began searching for her birth mother.

"She'd listen to me when I was frustrated. I'd call her and say, 'I didn't get a card or anything, I can't believe it!' Then I'd hang up and think, 'My God, is that ever nervy of me to phone her!'"

Jackie was encouraged by a friend who pointed out that although contact was minimal, her birth mother hadn't told her to stop writing or calling.

Although some adoptees do not have face-to-face meetings with their birth mother right away, patience often pays off. It can take several years before a birth mother is ready to meet with the adoptee. Nevertheless, a meeting that takes place after a wait of two, seven or however many years seems worthwhile, according to those who have waited. It's important to remember, if you're in the "limbo" stage, to be patient and respectful, and to realize that your birth mother may eventually agree to a reunion, but according to her own timetable, not yours.

THE BIRTH MOTHER'S EXPERIENCE

Ursula remembers her reunion with her birth son Stephen, when he was 21 years old. "For the first meeting, he came here. I was a nervous wreck, walking the floor and looking out the windows. The night before, I must have looked at every car that drove by our house."

Tina was 35 when she found her birth son, John, then aged 20. "The night before we met, I was awake all night. I had two pots of coffee and saw the sun come up. I met the paper boy at the door at seven in the morning. "I was thinking, should I buy 20 birthday cards, one for each year, and a whole bunch of balloons and show up at the door and go for funny? Ta-da! Should I give a little speech? What was I going to do?"

Tina lost five pounds during the week preceding her reunion. "I dissected everything," she remembers. "I really didn't know how he was going to react. I said to my friend, Ellen, 'What if John drives a motorcycle? What if he's a hood, or a down-and-out druggie who thinks, 'Ha! Struck it rich with these people!' You have to think of these things. And then when I met him, he *did* drive a motorcycle and he wore an earring!"

While Tina relied on friends and family for support before her reunion, she wanted privacy during the meeting itself. This is a common need among birth mothers.

Tina didn't even want Roger, her husband and John's birth father, to share her reunion. "This was something I was doing for me," she explains. "I said to Roger, 'It would probably be easier on John if he wasn't overwhelmed by both of us at once,' which was a big lie. I wanted him to myself."

Tina was also afraid that John wouldn't react the same way if her husband was present at the reunion.

COUNSELLING

Tina met her birth son through Parent Finders, but she did not receive pre-reunion counselling. Her experiences demonstrate the complex issues that reunions sometimes provoke. Because of the many uncertainties, expectations, fantasies and emotions involved in a reunion, counselling and/or education before the reunion is just as important for the birth mother as it is for the adoptee.

Adoption has denied birth mothers the growing-up years of their relinquished children. A reunion may reactivate many years' worth of repressed grief on the part of the birth mother. Until the possibility of a reunion arises, this unexpressed pain is buried within. When given the opportunity for a reunion, birth mothers view the meeting as a chance to begin bridging the years. But it's important to keep expectations realistic. Before a reunion, a counsellor can help to underscore the fact that those years will never be recaptured; scaled-down expectations allow the birth mother to grieve and to think about beginning her relationship with the adoptee in the present.

Birth mothers who were young, naive, alone and terrified at the time of the adoptee's birth and adoption may experience intense memories of that time as they anticipate the reunion. Counselling can help birth mothers to avoid becoming overwhelmed by these painful memories and feelings.

For those whose reunion is orchestrated by a social service agency, the memories can be all too palpable. The agency remains a frightening place for the birth mother, whose last dealings with it left her with empty arms and a wound that would never completely heal. It is not surprising, therefore, that many birth mothers feel "put out," if not resentful, towards mandatory or "highly recommended" counselling sessions at the agency where their child was originally taken from them.

While approaching her reunion date, birth mother Rosemary recalls telling her social worker, "I'm 37 years old, I can handle it. I thought, 'Who does she [the counsellor] think she is?'" Today, Rosemary is a member of a post-adoption reunion support group, which is run by the same social worker who conducted her reunion. Often reunitees realize the benefits of counselling only after their reunion has taken place.

CONCERNS OF THE BIRTH MOTHER

Many birth mothers fear finding a child who closely resembles the birth father. For birth mothers who don't subsequently marry the birth father, old wounds may be reopened by the prospect of a reunion with their birth child, someone who may be an exact replica of a man they've tried for many years to forget.

Joan is a social worker and a reunited adoptee. "I had a friend who was a birth mother and who was going to meet her birth daughter," remarks Joan. "She called me and said, 'Do you think she'll ask about her birth father?' I said, 'Yes, count on it. She will definitely ask.'"

Allowing the adoptee to control the reunion and its outcome is common among birth mothers because they feel that they made their choice long ago, so now they must leave the choices up to the adoptee. Birth mothers often feel that their rights and needs are secondary to those of the adoptee. They fear that the adoptee will "walk in" and "walk out" of their lives: this is a scenario that echoes their first meeting and parting, at the adoptee's birth. It also, in many cases, replicates the course of the relationship with the birth father.

My birth mother wrote before our reunion, "I'm glad you have reached out, even if it is just for facts. Only you can give me any rights, such as asking for a meeting."

Another reason birth mothers sometimes do not assert

themselves when they'd like to is the fear that the adoptee will be angry with them for "giving them up" for adoption.

Pat O'Brien is a social worker and assistant registrar at the Ministry of Community and Social Services in Toronto, Ontario, the ministry that houses the central adoption registry for that province. O'Brien has been involved in contacting birth mothers who have been located by the provincial registry, on behalf of adoptees. "In my experience," says O'Brien, "a number of birth parents, from early years on, feel that the adoptee is going to be angry with them, that they're not going to want to see them because they didn't raise them, that the adoptee hates them and that they, the birth parents, don't have the right to see the adoptee."

Counselling can help a birth mother to be better prepared for her reunion by letting her know that she can assert her own needs, thereby taking care of herself and ensuring a more balanced relationship with the adoptee.

Birth fathers also fear repercussions from a meeting with an adoptee. Especially when they have subsequently married the birth mother, the pangs of guilt can be overwhelming for the birth father. Before her reunion, Tina says, "Roger was excited for me and scared for himself." If the birth father had advocated abortion or pushed for the adoption, his guilt can be compounded when he is later confronted with a child who "shows up at the doorstep" for a meeting.

Birth parents also worry about the reactions of the adoptive parents towards the upcoming reunion.

"I was more concerned about the adoptive parents' feelings than I was about Joanne's," says Rosemary. "I thought, I can handle her, but I can't handle her adoptive parents."

Dealing with the adoptive parents may or may not become an issue after the actual meeting. But worries that adoptive parents will be jealous, offended or threatened strike fear in birth mothers, which augments their pre-reunion tension. This tension is understandable. Birth mothers who are having reunions today were given little respect, counselling, financial assistance or support when they relinquished their children, while the adoptive parents had all the legal rights to the child and were socially accepted. It is easy for a birth mother to feel that she is not on equal footing with the adoptive mother, given these circumstances.

While the birth mother knows she does not want to "replace" the adoptive mother, she may feel that she must somehow prove this to the adoptive mother. She may fear that she will not be accepted, that she will be treated as an unimportant stranger. Birth mothers were told to forget their child and to get on with their lives. They must ask themselves, "Will the adoptive parents be angry because I am no longer doing what I was told?" These are questions that only the reunion itself can answer.

TELLING SUBSEQUENT CHILDREN

Besides worrying about disturbing the adoptive family, birth parents have their own nuclear families to consider. One birth mother who had not revealed her "secret" of having a child prior to wedlock says, "There are so many people who would be ashamed of the birth mother. But there is only one adoptee to be disappointed if the reunion does not go well."

Birth mothers who are close to their children often report positive reactions from them when they are told about their "new" siblings.

Tina recalls talking with her middle son, David, about her upcoming reunion with John.

"David was 13, just coming into his sexuality. I thought, 'I can't tell him his mother did what I'm telling him not to do,'" explains Tina.

"We went downstairs, and Roger got a beer and offered David a freshie.

"Roger started off like a bedtime story, 'Now, David, your mommy and I have gone together since we were very young,' and I'm thinking, 'Jeez, Roger, the kid's not a baby,' and he went on, 'Well, you know, we had a little baby and we had to give him up for adoption.'

"And you found him, right?" David said.

"I told him that his brother was 20 and that he rode a motorcycle. David said, 'Awesome.'"

Children today don't hold the same negative stereotypes of single mothers as do their parents. With more women choosing single motherhood, more relaxed attitudes about sexuality, the rising divorce statistics resulting in single-parent homes and homes with stepbrothers and stepsisters, it's little wonder that most teens adapt quickly to their parent's (or parents') revelation.

A birth mother's husband who is not the birth father may also pose problems for the impending reunion. In fact, when the husband doesn't know about the relinquished child, as in Laura's case, a reunion may not take place at all. Or it may transpire in a secret place, remaining underground indefinitely.

THE ADOPTIVE PARENTS' EXPERIENCE

Louise and Frank were 54 years old when their son, Thomas, met his birth mother. Thomas was 26. Thomas's adoptive parents accompanied him to his birth mother's town at his request, and waited while he had his reunion. "Not knowing what was going on, wondering, surmising ... I couldn't have gone by myself, if it were me," states Louise.

"We didn't want to interfere. But it turned out all right. In fact, we thought he was never going to come back. He left about two in the afternoon and we didn't see him again until 11:30 that night. I just paced, wondering how things were going. I assumed since he didn't come back, things were going well. I had taken some crocheting and a book and tried to watch television. I don't think I accomplished any of these. It was the longest, hardest day that we'd ever put in."

Louise and Frank are unique in the degree of support they showed their adopted son before his reunion. There are still many adoptive parents who find out about the reunion only after it's over, if ever. When the adoptive parents know about the reunion beforehand, they prefer to stay in the background, in the majority of cases. A meeting between the adoptive parents and the birth mother is still quite uncommon.

FEELING THREATENED

Although the adoptive parents in this book have reported a positive adoption experience, most remember feeling threatened, to varying degrees, before their adopted son or daughter's reunion.

My own adoptive father said that while he didn't feel threatened by my meeting with my birth mother, he did feel slightly so when I met my birth father. This was because, he explained, he obviously could not be "replaced" by my birth mother, but he was a little less secure when I found another "father."

Paul had similar feelings before Lisa, his adopted daughter, met her birth mother. "She may find a replacement mother, but not a father, so I didn't feel threatened. When we adopted, he [the birth father] was already long gone," explains Paul.

Lisa's adoptive mother, Donna, remarks, "Your initial reaction, even though you expected it, is to feel slightly hurt, worrying that you couldn't give her enough. When she got angry, she'd say, 'You're not my real mother.' So it's obviously bothered her over the years that she was adopted. The hurt that she could never really accept us as her parents was overridden by the knowledge that this is what she needs. If she can find happiness, I think that's wonderful. We had no qualms other than a little twinge that it would be nice if she could have been more positive towards us as parents."

Although my father and I both knew he was irreplaceable to me, vulnerable feelings seem to arise whenever parents in a closed adoption feel their parenthood is challenged in any way. Fear of the unknown exacerbates these feelings. In the pre-reunion stage of a closed adoption, adoptive parents fear that the birth mother may, in fact, wish to "reclaim" her child, or to interfere in some way with the adoptive family. The fear that the birth mother will "come knocking" has lodged in their sub-conscious since the time of the adoption. The adoptive parents naturally wonder if all their fears about the reunion will also come true, and if their child will wish to spend more time with their birth family, rather than with the adoptive family.

It may be that, by its very nature, adoption lends itself to feelings of vulnerability on the part of the adoptive parents. While birth parents know they are "parents" by birth, adoptive parents are parents by law only. Perhaps they perceive this distinction as creating a more fragile parent-child bond. They may question whether their parenting has been "good enough." Before a reunion, adoptive parents' fears of their adequacy as parents may be heightened, and these fears sometimes manifest themselves as worry about being replaced by "better" parents.

THINGS TO REMEMBER

The pre-reunion stage is probably the most frightening part of a reunion. Fear of the unknown is a facet of human nature, and imaginations can run wild before the actual meeting. Here are a few tips to help you keep your feet on the ground and to survive the inevitable pre-reunion anxiety.

FOR THE ADOPTEE:

(1) Don't overplan.

(2) Don't rush into the reunion.

(3) Be good to yourself and get support. Professional counselling is an excellent idea.

(4) Maintain a positive self-image and a healthy independence. You will still have your job, your family and your kids after your reunion. Life will go on.

(5) Be ready to look like your birth mother. Also be ready to look nothing like her. Be ready to look like someone she loves or someone she loathes.

(6) Be realistic; remember no other birth relative besides your birth mother may know about you. If they do, they may not want to meet you.

(7) Regardless of what happens, you will have learned a lot.

FOR THE BIRTH MOTHER:

(1) Don't overplan.

(2) Monitor the pacing of your reunion.

(3) Be good to yourself and get support. Professional counselling is an excellent idea.

(4) Maintain a positive self-image and a healthy independence. Your life will continue as it has in the past.

(5) Be ready to answer lots of questions, including those about the birth father.

(6) Regardless of what happens, you will have learned a lot.

FOR THE ADOPTIVE PARENTS:

(1) Try to offer support without prying.

(2) Remember that the adoptee is an adult. This is her reunion, not yours, unless you are invited.

FOR ALL:

(1) Be aware of your fantasies and fears. Try to keep them both to a minimum.

§

CHAPTER 8

YOU'RE ON:
THE REUNION

Cathy opened the door, revealing a slender woman clad in a light-blue jean skirt and jacket. She had short, dark hair and hazel eyes. The woman rose, reached out her arms and my armour dissolved; we wordlessly embraced, tears streaming down our faces. We held one another for a few moments, and in those moments, through the feeling shared between us, I knew she was my birth mother, and the amazement of this awed me into silence.

After our embrace, she handed me a rose. I laughed and told her of my plan to bring her one and of my fears that had kept me from doing so. "Well, we'll share this one, then," she said.

—M. M.

MANY OF US cry at weddings, funerals and even college graduations. Just as these momentous occasions signify "rites of passage," so too is a post-adoption reunion a rite of passage. Like any major life change, it is a turning point, and with it comes a release of emotion and a launch into uncharted waters.

The issues and experiences for birth mothers and adoptees differ, but many feelings and reactions overlap. Who wouldn't be terrified at the first glimpse of their birth child or birth mother in 20, 30 or 40 years? How do you start the conversation: "Hi, how've you been these past 20 years?"

At a graduation ceremony, the moment the diploma hits your palm, you have symbolically received a vast amount of knowledge. During a reunion, adoptees and birth mothers receive a crash-course in each other's lives, cramming as many details as possible into one hour, one afternoon or one day. The reunion leaves the "graduate" exhausted, disappointed or elated; but always changed forever.

Because "re-union" is exactly that — a meeting between two parties who have met before — this chapter will discuss only the issues for the participants of the reunion, the adoptee and the birth mother. Those adoptive parents who do meet birth family members rarely meet them at the same time as the adoptee. It is far more common for them to meet the birth mother in the same week or, more commonly, several months after the adoptee first makes contact. We'll discuss what it's like for adoptive parents to meet birth parents in Chapters 9 and 10.

THE ADOPTEE'S EXPERIENCE

The minutes before the actual meeting can be the most emotional ones in an adoptee's life. Gord, an adoptee who met his birth mother when he was 19, had only two thoughts moments before his reunion: that he would either go through with it or that he would run away.

After Gord's adoptive mother had driven him to the building where he was to meet his birth mother for the first time as an adult, he remembers thinking, "By this time, I knew my mother was in the building. It was like, Elvis is in the building, right? I was severely nauseous. I thought I was going to vomit. I was terrified."

Sharon, Gord's social worker, led him to a room and opened the door. "I thought, 'Alright, either I'm going to turn in there, and I'm going to look at my birth mother and all my questions will be answered; or I'm going to turn around and run like hell and forget I ever wanted to do this. And I started to pivot. I thought, 'Where the hell is the door out?' But I stuck my head around the corner, and there she was."

"Right away, she stood up and started to cry," continues Gord. "She said, 'Can I touch you?' And I said, 'Yes, I guess so.' I was still in the doorway. I was terrified. Then I suppose I stepped in and she gave me a hug, but it was strange. I felt like I was hugging my birth mother. I was conscious of that, but I didn't feel a bond right away; that came later. Then we sat down. By this point, I had started to cry too."

Adoptees should be prepared, as in Gord's case, for the birth mother's need for physical contact. This may be awkward when others, such as family members or a social worker, are present.

Anne is an adoptee who met her birth brother, Douglas, when she was 32 years old and Douglas was 28. Anne had been adopted before her birth parents married. A year later, they married and gave birth to Douglas, whom they raised as an only child. They subsequently divorced. When Douglas was 27 years old, he learned about Anne when he discovered her birth certificate among his parents' documents. He began a search immediately.

Anne remembers the day of her reunion: "Douglas sat at one end of the table. I sat at the other and Meg [the social worker] sat in the middle. And nobody said anything," says Anne. Meg clued in and went for coffee, shutting the door behind her. Then, Anne and Douglas embraced and cried. They later went to her birth father's home, where she met her birth father Chris and his wife Janice.

"They were all watching us as we hugged," says Anne. "And I thought, 'Oh, God, I don't need this.'" Anne felt very uncomfortable being "on display" at her reunion.

When hugs and crying have subsided, photographs and stories are usually shared. My birth mother remained silent as we looked at my family photos, asking only a brief question or two. I think we were both stunned as we sat in each other's presence. It was more than we'd ever had and it was overwhelming.

Usually, both adoptees and birth mothers bring photographs of their families to their reunion. But it's the adoptee who's hoping to uncover the mystery of her past, so it's more often the birth mother who shares photographs and tells stories during the reunion. In fact, the adoptee may find that discussing her life and her adoptive family may leave them both feeling vulnerable.

"I was very close to my adoptive grandparents," says Gord. "When I showed Vicky [Gord's birth mother] a picture of them, I was very emotional. I was saying, 'These are really special, important people to me.' It was my own little defense mechanism."

As my birth mother and I pored over the photos, I told her that my adoptive father had wanted to come with me when I met her. "Where does he live?" she asked.

"Kitchener," I replied.

"Well, why don't we go meet him, then?" she suggested.

So, at three in the afternoon, we took our reunion on the road!

My adoptive father's tearful embrace told her she was welcome. He accepted her the same way he had raised me, with openness, honesty and a warm heart. He thanked her for giving me life, and for his and my adoptive mother's opportunity to raise me. We sat around the fireplace going through boxes and boxes of photographs. I felt like the star in an episode of "This is Your Life." I was both flattered and embarrassed, as my childhood, teenage years and adulthood were paraded before my birth mother.

I felt sorry for my sister Melissa, who sat through all this having so recently lost our mother (her birth mother). Melissa seemed pleased, though, to meet my birth mother and she was accepting of my reunion.

Sometimes adoptees receive gifts, as well as stories and photographs, at their reunion. My birth mother had brought other gifts besides a rose: family photos and a tiny pair of gold sewing scissors shaped like a crane. But the best gifts were the answers to some of the questions I'd had all my life.

Vicky's family bought Gord an expensive watch that Gord now wears every day. "They bought it for me when they learned that Vicky was going to meet me. It was to welcome me into the family."

CONCERNS OF THE ADOPTEE

Perhaps the gesture of a gift helps to smooth over other aspects of the reunion that are more difficult for an adoptee.

"Vicky's mother kept lifting her glasses down and staring at me, not meaning to. She couldn't help herself," says Gord. Looking for physical and personality similarities is a natural reaction during a reunion.

"I just eyed him up and down," says Anne of her meeting with her birth father. "I knew right off that he was my dad. I look a lot like him. I have dark skin too."

After Gord and Vicky left the Children's Aid office where they had met, they drove to a restaurant and talked and talked. "We just got to know each other, like, 'Who are you and what have you done?' What's similar and what's not similar? When you get on that one-to-one basis, you start looking for similarities."

Adoptees should be aware that some of these similarities may be painful for their birth relatives. Gord remembers the time he and Vicky went to visit his paternal birth grandparents. Gord's birth father Jeff had died in an accident shortly after Gord was born.

"Jeff's sister and her children were there," says Gord. "Three or four of them started crying because I looked so much like Jeff. They couldn't believe it. It was like a miracle to them because Jeff has been dead for 20 years and in walks his son.

"They took me to Jeff's bedroom, which has virtually remained the same since he'd been killed. I said, 'Just let me stay here for a while,' and I asked them all to leave. All of it was so overwhelming."

And there Gord found a treasure trove of family memorabilia. On the shelves in his father's old room were trophies won by Jeff, as well as photographs and books he had read.

One of the reasons adoptees can be overwhelmed by their reunion is the fact that they are frequently outnumbered. While there is only one adoptee, there may be many birth family members and their friends to meet at one time.

Robert met his birth family at a large family party thrown by his birth mother's relatives. "There must have been 40 to 50 people there," says Emily, Robert's birth mother. "He stuck to me like glue that day. The host's son and all his buddies were there, and they were all the same age as Robert. I said to them, 'You guys try to make Robert feel comfortable.' "

A competent D.J., Robert played a song and dedicated it to his birth mother and they danced. "The whole family stood around and watched us and cried. It was scary for Robert. Coming into a family this size was very difficult. He had many people to meet, but I just had to get acquainted with him," she says.

Emily's family welcomed Robert, but felt protective towards Emily. This also added to Robert's discomfort.

Sometimes, instead of meeting a lot of new people at your reunion, you may be surprised to learn that you already know some of your birth family members or their friends. This may happen especially when the birth family and the adoptive family live in the same town or area. One adoptee met his birth parents — whom he'd known as his next-door neighbours for more than 30 years!

"I used to get kidded at school that I was a brother to the kids next door — and I was!" laughs this adoptee.

Having things in common may serve to ease the tension, but dissimilarities in personality, upbringing or values will invariably cause minor to major difficulties.

Anne's birth father is Greek, but Anne was not raised by a Greek family. When Anne met him, "His custom was to eat, eat, eat. He got mad because I wasn't eating anything. But I was too scared to eat."

Adjusting to different family or ethnic customs is just one source of discomfort for the adoptee meeting her birth family for the first time.

Anne learned that the background information she had been given by her social worker was nothing like the reality. Anne's birth mother later told her that she had named a platonic friend as the birth father. This revelation added to the emotional impact of the siblings' reunion.

"The day Douglas and I met," says Anne, "he said, 'I am not your half-brother. I am your full brother. My dad is your dad and always will be.'" Anne later verified this information.

Anne reacted to her first meeting with her birth mother by asking "a million" questions about her background, which is a typical reaction. However, she was disappointed because she felt there was a lot her birth mother wasn't telling her at their reunion.

Most adoptees want information about their birth. It's quite a shock, after waiting years for a reunion, to find that your birth mother does not remember the details of your birth and relinquishment. Yet this is a common phenomenon. Because of the trauma of the adoption, many birth mothers have repressed the very information the adoptee so fervently seeks through the reunion. Some birth mothers even forget their child's birth date. Adoptees should be forewarned of this possible loss of memory. Hopefully, as the reunion progresses, a safe environment and a good relationship between the birth mother and the adoptee will help the birth mother to unearth her story and to share it with the adoptee.

OVERLOAD

Before I met my birth mother, I wondered how I would ask the questions I most needed to ask. My inquiries were so personal and intimate, and she was a complete stranger. But, I thought, this might be my only chance. I needed to know: Where was my birth father? What happened between them? Why was I given up for adoption? So many people had given me shreds of information that, I knew, only approximated the truth. I now had the chance to hear it from the only person who knew what had actually happened.

During our initial meeting, the social worker left us alone to talk. And in the next two hours, my birth mother shared so much, I could hardly retain it all. I sat quietly while she spoke.

My birth mother seemed anxious to make up for the past, to explain herself to me. She, too, had waited a long time for this meeting.

Although my nervousness had chased away my appetite, after two hours of conversation, we left the Children's Aid building to have lunch in a nearby restaurant. What I ordered or what we said is now a blur. We basked in our emotions and when it was time to leave, I suggested going to my apartment so I could show her where I lived and some of my photographs. I didn't want to let her go.

Rushing to learn everything about their background as fast as possible is a mistake commonly made by adoptees. Like cramming for a school exam, it's not a great idea. And, just like cramming for exams, you'll probably forget everything you "learned" within days.

When Anne met Douglas, "I was like a sponge," she recalls. "'Feed me more, more information.' I was trying to get the whole thing, everything, at once."

In spite of the adoptees' insatiable craving for information, they sometimes find that their birth mothers are reluctant to share details about the birth father or the adoption. Although this may be frustrating for the adoptee, it's best not to try to push for facts in the early stage of the relationship. Focussing on what is offered is probably a much better tactic. There will certainly be enough to absorb from one meeting without asking for more right away.

Just as you may be overloaded with information on your first meeting with your birth mother, you may also be tempted to meet other birth relatives on the same day.

Gord's birth mother, Vicky, asked him if he wanted to meet her family after their reunion. Gord jumped at the chance, and agreed to meet them that night after he finished work.

Gord and Vicky drove to various birth relatives' homes to introduce Gord to his "new" family. "At every house we went to, I was nervous. Her sister was smothering me with hugs and kisses and stuff, and it felt really strange."

Both Gord and Anne agree that they would take their reunions "a heck of a lot slower," if they had to do it all again. While unscheduled meetings with additional family members may go smoothly, they inevitably compound the reunion day burnout. There are simply too many details to absorb.

Because adoptees have lived for so many years with little or no information about their birth families, their curiosity and their need drives them to collect so much information so quickly. With each new reunion, more insight is gained by the adoptee into her own identity. Wanting to meet increasing numbers of birth family members, even though the original and ultimate goal was to meet her birth mother, is evidence of the depth of the adoptee's primal need to solidify her identity.

Although adoptees may not feel pressured into meeting more relatives, many of us are eager to please and emotionally vulnerable on the day of our reunion. Adoptees are especially fearful of rejection. So when a birth mother says, "Would you like to?" it's sometimes difficult for an adoptee to say no, even if she would rather not do something.

Reunions are disorienting events, with all the new people to meet and so much information to absorb. Gord had to go to work the afternoon he met his birth mother. Like many adoptees, he couldn't concentrate at all on the day of his reunion.

"You should have seen me," says Gord. "Anybody I told the story to, cried. I was so emotional, people would say, 'Don't tell me any more, I can't handle it.'"

All this activity sometimes leads to depression and/or exhaustion later on. Anne, a mother of three, compares her feeling at the conclusion of her reunion to post-partum depression.

"It's like after you have a baby. You're really happy, but it's all over with. It's the post-reunion blues."

Although Anne had told her whole family about her reunion, once it was over, she just wanted to be alone. Anne asked her husband to take her calls. She needed to recuperate.

"I knew what my brother looked like. I'd learned the family background and I wanted to see more of him. I wanted to find out everything. But my emotions were just drained once I finally met him," Anne remembers.

SEPARATION ANXIETY

Two years after I met my birth father, I met his other daughter. We had exchanged several letters, but when we finally met, she was painfully shy. I was overwhelmed; she was intelligent, beautiful, and she was my sister! When we hugged goodbye after our meeting, I was beset by a deep sadness. I burst into tears instantly as I watched her go. A fear clouded my heart: would I ever see her again? I felt a deep loss, which wove the present and the past together in a shroud and covered my happiness. Our sisterhood had never been ... but could it ever be?

The feelings of loss, emptiness and near-panic on saying goodbye to a newly found birth relative are common ones for adoptees. Separation is never easy. For adoptees, the initial separation from their birth mother, father or siblings was expected to be final. The adoptee has lingering fears, then, that perhaps this goodbye might actually be the last.

THE BIRTH MOTHER'S EXPERIENCE

At age 20, birth mother Karen relinquished her newborn daughter.

"I never went to bed at night without thinking about her," recalls Karen.

"My first reaction when she contacted me was, 'Thank God, she's okay.'" When Karen first met her daughter, Susan, then 24, she just wanted to know that she was "real" and that she was all right, Karen says.

Birth mothers need to explain the circumstances of the adoption and many yearn to be forgiven for their decision to relinquish. Tina describes it in these terms: "I think it's a common compulsion of birth mothers: the first thing you have to tell your kid is that they weren't an unwanted child. They were loved and wanted, by their mothers if nobody else. Otherwise, we could have aborted."

Of her meeting five years ago with Joanne, her birth daughter, Rosemary says, "All I wanted was her forgiveness. I wanted her to say, 'I don't hold anything against you, I understand why you did what you did.' And she hasn't said it to this day."

Before explanations can be made, however, the reunion path has to be cleared of pent-up emotions.

The day she met her birth son, who was then 21 years old, Tina waited at her sister's house for her son's arrival. "Then I heard his motorcycle," says Tina. "My feet didn't even touch the ground. I was suddenly standing there in front of him, my finger in my mouth, like I did when I was a little kid, looking at him like an idiot. He'd barely gotten his helmet off and I just jumped on him. I didn't even get a good look at him.

"I could feel him shaking and he was hugging me back really hard." Both John and Tina were speechless; she was in tears, he was on the verge of tears.

"That night I stayed at his place," says Tina. "We sat on the couch and I held him while he cried. I said, 'Go ahead, John, let it out. It's been a long time coming.' "

HOLDING YOUR CHILD

Holding and touching their children are strong needs for most birth mothers.

At her first Parent Finders meeting following her reunion with John, Tina mentioned to one of the members that she couldn't keep her hands off her son when they first met. "All I wanted to do was touch him, just hear him breathe," says Tina. The woman in whom Tina had confided said, "That's because he's a boy." Tina felt very uncomfortable with that remark.

The reason for Tina's discomfort was the implication of

sexual attraction between herself and her son. Although this was not the case with Tina and her son, social workers and reunitees do report the phenomenon of sexual attraction occurring between reunited family members. This is referred to as "Genetic Sexual Attraction" or GSA.[23]

Social worker Cathy Basile explains how sexual attraction may develop between reunited siblings. A similar mechanism can also operate between birth parents and their offspring.

"When you're growing up with your brothers and sisters," says Basile, "you know that they're your brothers and sisters. You have fights with them, you know they throw their socks around. When you suddenly meet a person who may have many of the same characteristics that you have and who looks like you, obviously there's an attraction.

"Because the incest taboo has not been in place over the years, however, and being the human animals that we are, the attraction that we feel can become sexual. In your head, you know that there is a biological affiliation, but on an emotional level, you don't. It's a brand new relationship, so you don't yet know how to deal with it."

For those who conduct their reunions through a social agency, counselling about this delicate aspect should be included when discussing the many issues that arise during the course of a reunion. Basile says most reunitees are initially shocked at the mention of GSA. However, she believes that most of her clients are mature enough to be able to cope with these strange and unsettling feelings, especially when they've been forewarned of the possibility.

"When they do experience sexual attraction," says Basile, "and I think many of them do, they can put it into perspective and recognize it for what it is."

Another explanation for the need to touch one another during a reunion, explains Basile, is that most birth mothers only saw their children when they were very young. Their experience with their child was mainly a physical connection. It was touching, cuddling and cooing. So when they suddenly meet their offspring as adults, they go back to what they last knew with their child — they start touching them again. Tina concurs with this explanation.

"To me," says Tina, "this was my baby, and I treated him like a baby. I compare it with when you first bring a baby home. Everyone says 'Who does he look like? He's got so-and-so's eyes; his ears are like so-and-so's. You gather around a baby and you ogle. Well, that's what we did to John. Only he was grown up."

Karen also recalls her need to touch her daughter at their first meeting.

"It really bothered me that I would occasionally reach out and put my hand on hers and she pulled back," says Karen. But Karen says that it was probably difficult for her birth daughter Susan, because she was very self-conscious.

THE BIRTH FATHER

But what if your child looks like the birth father? Someone, perhaps, that you'd rather forget. Understandably, some birth mothers have difficulty discussing the birth father at their reunion, whether their relationship with the birth father continued or ended abruptly.

Fuelled by the fear of rejection, birth mothers often tend to "give too much" of themselves at their first meeting, only to regret it later. Birth mothers should remember that it's okay to give only what they're emotionally prepared to give at their reunion.

On the day of her reunion, Joanne asked her birth mother why she'd been "given away" and about her birth father.

"I wasn't prepared for that question that day," recollects Rosemary, "because I'd heard that it was later on that they asked, not the day they met you. I just said, 'I'm not prepared to talk about him at this time, Joanne.' I said that I wasn't married and I didn't have family support. I didn't go into detail. It sufficed for a while."

For some birth mothers, the story of their child's birth father doesn't pose any particular problems, and so they feel comfortable retelling it.

"I told my birth son about his father," says Ursula. "I told him a lot at that first meeting."

DEALING WITH NEIGHBOURS AND FRIENDS

In spite of the intimacy of a reunion, many birth mothers are subjected to the scrutiny of others during their meeting.

Karen's birth daughter, Susan, had a friend come to visit the day of their reunion. Susan's friend said to Karen, "My God, how did you ever live through it? Twenty-five years and you never knew where she was." Comments like this do little to ease the tension of a reunion.

Karen's reunion was over 1,500 miles away from her home. "I was frightened and nervous by the end of the day," says Karen. "If I had been able to go and meet my daughter, have our reunion, then go home, it would have been great. But I was there for two weeks, come hell or high water, whether I liked these people or not."

The bombardment of irrational worries that plague a nervous birth mother throughout her first meeting is one reason why reunions are so exhausting. The flip-flop back and forth from exultation to fear also contributes to the emotional burnout experienced at the reunion's conclusion.

"I felt, 'I finally did it!'" says Ursula of her reunion. "I got this far and did what I wanted to do. But now I was worried about what was coming next. I wondered how to approach my son and make him love me and care about me." These thoughts nagged at Ursula throughout her reunion, as her birth son, whom she hadn't seen in 21 years, sat beside her.

"It was difficult to start a conversation," remembers Ursula, "but I did, and then just talked away. I talked an awful lot, which I realized, even at the time, was just because of nerves."

The paradox of a reunion is that it is both the coveted end of a long search and a heartfelt desire, and the beginning of a whole new life. Most reunitees begin to realize, by the end of their reunion day, that life will never be the same again.

THINGS TO REMEMBER

A reunion is a rite of passage. It's a tumultuous, trying, terrific event. You've gotten this far. You deserve to be kind to yourself and to savour the moment. Here are some tips to help you do that.

FOR THE ADOPTEE:

(1) Try not to meet your entire genetic lineage of the past four generations in one afternoon. Remember to pace your experience.

(2) Expect to feel "abandoned" after the reunion is over.

(3) If your adoptive parents know about your reunion, check in with them. Let them know you're okay.

(4) If your reunion is out of town, don't stay with your birth mother. She'll need her time alone. So will you.

(5) Don't expect your birth mother to have vivid memories and remember every detail. She might; she might not. Give her time.

(6) Give yourself time off after the reunion to get settled with your own emotions.

FOR THE BIRTH MOTHER:

(1) Don't introduce your whole family to the adoptee in one day. There are lots of birth relatives, only one adoptee. Try not to overwhelm your child. It's okay to be the star for the day.

(2) Treat yourself to a hotel if your reunion is out-of-town. You'll need the privacy to absorb your feelings and recharge your batteries.

FOR THE ADOPTIVE PARENTS:

(1) If you don't hear from the adoptee, don't assume they've abandoned you. Don't assume the reunion was horrible. Don't assume anything.

(2) Try to be patient.

FOR ALL:

(1) As always, get support.

(2) Give yourself some extra care and attention. Take the day off work, unplug the phone, go for a massage or just go back to bed. Relax.

(3) Try to remember that everyone else is probably as nervous and frightened as you are. Be compassionate.

§

CHAPTER 9

POST REUNION: SHORT-TERM ISSUES

For me, the peak emotional experience has passed — we've met. Now that the reunion is over I can count on my friends, family and social worker to take an interest in how things are going and to support me. I realize that for my birth mother, her sole support has been her husband, since she's shared her deepest secret only with him. For her, our meeting has created many complications.

My birth mother and I continue our visits and correspondence. During the first six months after our reunion, we were filled with nervousness and tension. Slowly, we have become more relaxed. But I often wonder if the fear that we may lose one another in the next moment will ever totally wear off.

— M. M.

THE TIME FROM the initial contact to up to 12 months following the reunion is commonly referred to as the "honeymoon" period. This blissful stage is not without its difficulties, but the problems inherent in the honeymoon period are quite different from those that beset the long-term post-reunion phase. This chapter deals with the short-term issues associated with initial stages of post reunion, and Chapter 10 addresses the somewhat more complex issues that arise when the first "high" of the reunion has worn off.

Like the aftermath of a long-planned-for wedding, reunitees settle in after their reunion day to the reality of their "marriage" to one another. After the first shock of the reunion diminishes, there are many immediate issues to deal with. While problematic, these concerns are nonetheless permeated by the heady euphoria of the recent reunion.

Just as in married life, most of the difficulties and concerns come as a surprise. Reunitees are ill-prepared for the aftermath of their meeting, for several reasons. First, most adoptees are focussed on the excitement of finally meeting their birth mother, giving very little thought to the outcome of the meeting, except in general terms: Will she like me? Will I like her? and so on. Second, reunited counterparts are virtual strangers to each other and they often have very little information about one another prior to their meeting. Finally, there are no established models for post-reunion relationships. Reunitees must create their own definitions of who they are in relation to one another.

THE ADOPTEE'S EXPERIENCE

In the first months following my reunion with my birth mother, there were many letters and phone calls between us as our "honeymoon" period ensued. It was during this stage that I struggled to replace my fantasy mother with the flesh and blood human being I'd met. It wasn't easy. We were both eager to please, anxious to learn about one another, and lost as to how to proceed. What sort of relationship would we have? There were so many mysteries ahead.

The first weekend I visited my birth mother's house, champagne corks popped. I was treated like royalty, as the secret was shared with friends and family. Gifts of flowers were showered upon me. I was totally unprepared for and overwhelmed by such a reception.

But not all of my initial experiences as part of my birth mother's life were positive. At a dance with her and her husband, I was introduced to an even wider circle of their acquaintances and old friends. One woman pronounced, with her finger pointed at my face, "That's not your daughter. You don't have a daughter." I was already feeling vulnerable and her comment triggered a deep embarrassment and humiliation within me. I suppose this woman was shocked by the news, but I resented her insensitivity.

OBSESSION

Having a reunion is like suddenly going off a strict diet and being offered a chocolate mousse cake. It's impossible to resist the temptation to "overindulge" in the new relationship that you've been craving for years.

"I was absorbing so much information, I didn't want it to stop," says Gord. "It all seemed so convenient. My birth mother lived a five-minute drive away from me. She had never married, had no other kids, so she felt unthreatened. I was virtually her only blood relative.

"After we met, I phoned her every day on my work breaks, or she phoned me. I'd say, 'Hi. Do you want me to stop by after work?' and she'd say, 'Come by, come by.' I think there were two or three months of that. There was a lot of seeing each other, getting to know each other."

Anne remembers her initial relationship with her birth sibling, Douglas. "At the beginning, it was great. I could look at Douglas and he could look at me and we'd each know what the other was thinking. We saw each other every day. In fact, my husband was getting angry because I was seeing Douglas all the time instead of him."

After the first weekend at my birth mother's home, it took a long time to catch my breath. Having met so many new people and faced so much curiosity, I needed privacy to assimilate all I'd felt and learned. Where would I place these people in my life? I was introduced as my birth mother's "daughter." I had to let this idea sink in. What did "daughter" mean in our case?

FAMILY JEALOUSIES

Obsession with your newly found birth relatives can create feelings of jealousy in those around you. Anne's relationship with her brother Douglas was very close for the first ten months after they'd been reunited. Anne and Douglas saw each other "just about every day," recalls Anne.

"Now, all of a sudden, he's too busy. He had put me on a big pedestal when we first met. It's hard to come down from it."

Douglas had been raised an only child. After Anne met her birth mother, Carol, Douglas's attitude seemed to change.

"I went to see Carol for a couple of days in the summer," says Anne. "It went fine, but Douglas got angry with me because he's never had to share anybody.

"I wondered what I had done to offend him. But he wouldn't tell me. When I asked, 'Is there anything wrong?' he said, 'No.'"

Douglas was also jealous of Anne's relationship with their father. Each time Anne received a gift from her birth father, Douglas was on the phone "one-upping" her by describing gifts he had also received from his dad.

Anne, who is two years older than Douglas, thought, "This little brother is getting to be a pain. He seemed like a mature person when I met him and now he's acting like a kid.

"I'm close to both his birth dad and his birth mother, and I think he takes offense to that. This sibling rivalry didn't come out until after our reunion."

Anne's husband became jealous when she spent a lot of time with Douglas. Douglas became jealous when she received gifts from their dad; and, as it turned out, Anne's birth mother became jealous when Douglas lessened his contact with her to spend more time with Anne.

Anne's predicament testifies to the benefits of having an experienced counsellor to rely on throughout the post-reunion process. "If I hadn't gone to counselling, I think my relationship with Douglas would have been over a long time ago," reflects Anne.

Adoptees may also find that their half-siblings, who are usually much younger than they are, may suffer jealousy in the initial stages of the reunion. If the birth mother's subsequent children do not know about the adoptee, the second-born child will grow up thinking she was the first-born. After the reunion, this child may feel displaced by the adoptee and experience confusion as she struggles to redefine her role in her family, just as the adoptee must struggle to establish herself with her birth mother and newfound siblings. Jealousy among siblings will probably be a short-lived reaction to the reunion as the siblings adjust to each other. The majority of adoptees say that they are well-accepted by their siblings, and often develop close friendships with them over time.

SOURCES OF FRUSTRATION
WITH YOUR BIRTH MOTHER

A common post-reunion complaint from many adoptees is the experience of being "babied" by their birth mothers. Gifts of teddy bears and dolls seem incongruous to a 28-year-old reunitee who has a family of her own. Some embarrassment or resentment might be felt by the adoptee.

As described in Chapter 8, many birth mothers feel compelled to touch their offspring during their reunion. Following up on the reunion by treating the adoptee as a baby or a young child is an extension of this reaction. The adoptee was in all likelihood a baby when the birth mother last saw her. It is this memory that is imprinted indelibly in her memory, and it may take some time, understanding and negotiation to bring the birth mother up to the present.

Sometimes, however, this "babying" can be just what the adoptee needs, at least for a while. Adoptees who had a difficult upbringing may crave the mothering they were deprived of as children.

Adoptees have usually been their birth mother's deep, dark secret until the reunion. Feelings of frustration, anger and hurt on the part of the adoptee often stem from the birth mother's refusal to "come out of the closet" about her reunion. An adoptee can feel rejected and slighted when her birth mother refuses to tell her husband, children and other family members about her child. It also makes it awkward for the adoptee to meet others in the birth family.

Sometimes, however, the stigma of secrecy is still not lifted, even following the reunion, if the reunion is cloaked in the same robe of disreputableness that tainted the adoption itself. One reunited adoptee met her birth mother secretly, in a town half-way between their respective residences. "It feels like we're sneaking around, like it's something wrong or shameful that we're doing," she comments.

Another adoptee lamented that her only contact with her birth mother was at her place of work. This environment limited conversation and impeded relationship-building.

It's important to remember that time eventually eases emotional pain. Patience is the key; it might take months or years for the birth mother to feel comfortable enough to reveal her "secret." Or she may never do so.

Even when an adoptee is acknowledged by her birth parents and introduced to other family members, anger may surface. Anne's "anger-trigger" came several months after her reunion with Chris, her birth father. For the first time since she'd met him, she thought, "He didn't want me 32 years ago. Why does he want me now?" It was Anne's birthday and Anne decided not to attend the party her birth father had planned for her.

"That day I was angry," remembers Anne. "I'd been over many times before, but when my birthday arrived, that was it. Chris called and said, 'What am I going to do with all this stuff?' I said, 'I don't care.' After that I calmed down and thought, 'This is ridiculous, I have to go out and talk to him.' Up until then we'd had a good relationship. I guess my anger had been all bottled up.

"When I got there, I said, 'You didn't want me 32 years ago, why do you want me now?' I said it to his face."

Another source of frustration for the reunited adoptee is "birth mother amnesia." The traumatic experience of giving birth to and then relinquishing a baby left deep scars for most birth mothers, scars that never healed. For this reason, much of the birth mother's memory of the birth and adoption may have been repressed and is apparently non-existent by the time the reunion rolls around. This creates a serious dilemma for the adoptee, who longs to hear the story of her birth and beginnings. This desire, in fact, may have been the initial impetus to pursue a reunion.

When my birth mother told me she couldn't remember my birth, I felt cheated and let down. At first, I didn't believe her and felt angry and confused. I couldn't understand, at that point, how someone could actually forget the experience of giving birth to a child. I had a lot to learn. I kept my anger inside, for fear of losing contact with my mother. Ironically, the day we met she told me she had registered because she felt she had a responsibility to answer any questions I might have!

As my reunion progressed and I matured, I began to understand what she'd been through and realized that she wasn't lying to me. She actually couldn't remember. My reunion is now four years old, and I still yearn for the details. I long to replace the "agency" story with a real "birth" day. I haven't given up hope.

TELLING YOUR ADOPTIVE PARENTS

For adoptees who have had an open relationship with their adoptive families, telling their parents about their reunion and its aftermath may not be an issue. For those who have experienced difficulties in their adoptive family — including their adoptive family's open hostility to the birth family or to the idea of a reunion — revealing their reunion may provoke conflict within the family. It may come as a shock, especially if family members are unaccustomed to expressing their feelings with each other. Sometimes even adoptees who say they are close to their adoptive parents choose not to share their reunion with their adoptive family.

"I lied to my adoptive parents," says Gord, who had just turned 19 when he met Vicky, his birth mother.

"I didn't tell them I was going to see Vicky for the first little while. I wanted it to be a year down the road when I could say, 'See? Everything's the same.' There was still no open conversation about it at my house, none that I remember. We did discuss my reunion, but it wasn't, 'Let's sit down and discuss this,' just, 'What happened?'

"I said, maybe twice, 'If you want to meet Vicky, I'll set something up. If you don't want to meet her, hey, that's fine.'" About a year after his reunion, Gord's adoptive mother asked Gord to invite Vicky over to meet Gord's adoptive family during the Christmas season.

Anne also waited until her reunion was over to tell her adoptive mother about it. Like Gord, Anne felt she would have to provide reassurance to her adoptive mother.

"I phoned my [adoptive] mom a few days after I'd met Douglas," says Anne. "I thought, 'I'd better tell her now, in case somebody says something through the grapevine.' I called her and said, 'There's something I'd like to tell you alone.' I went over there and was really nervous. I thought, 'How am I going to begin?'

"I said, 'I have a surprise. I found my brother. Well, he's found me, actually.' And I showed her the pictures and she started to cry.

"I said, 'Look at it this way, now you have another son. You're not losing me; far from it. It's just that I've found my brother.'

"A couple of days later," says Anne, "she [her adoptive mother] called me and said, 'You know, you're right. You had the right to know and everything's fine.' She wanted to meet him."

MOM, MEET MOM

For adoptees who see their birth mother every day (as is common in the "honeymoon" period), it's pretty awkward when you haven't figured out what to call her.

Anne has met both her birth mother and her birth father, in addition to her birth sibling, Douglas. "I call them mom and dad," says Anne. "I called them that right away. They said to call them whatever I want. I've never been one to call people who are older than me by their first name. Calling my dad 'Chris' or my mother 'Carol' wouldn't feel right. Here's Douglas [Anne's birth brother] calling his mom 'mom,' and here I am calling her 'Carol.' I didn't feel right about that."

Time may change how adoptees address their birth mother.

Depending on how the relationship develops, adoptees may call their birth mothers "mom" or use their first name, or they may move from a first-name basis to calling them "mom," as they become more comfortable with one another.

Sometimes adoptees juggle labels. They'll call their birth mother "mom" when they are speaking in private, and when they are in the company of their adoptive mother, they'll address their birth mother by her first name or they'll not refer to her by name at all. Most adoptees dance around the name issue in an effort not to offend or hurt their adoptive families.

Even when my own reunion was three years old, every time I thought about writing to my birth grandmother, I stopped short at "Dear...." Dear what? Dear Grandmother? Dear Anna? I've been so afraid of offending her, I haven't written yet. When we meet in person, as we have on three occasions, I don't need to worry about what to call her. Slowly, I'm getting to know her better. I feel loved and welcomed every time I see her, and now feel confident enough to ask her how I should begin my letters.

The only way to know what's comfortable for your birth relative and to let her know how you're feeling is through open dialogue, but sometimes it takes courage to broach difficult or sensitive subjects. And with respect to reunions, many areas are difficult and sensitive.

UNLEASHING AN ABUSIVE PAST

Some adoptees' ultimate dream is the reunion. Adoptees who have been removed from abusive homes, however, find that their dream can quickly turn into a nightmare. Besides the issues outlined above, these adoptees must deal with the extra layer of reactivating their painful beginnings. While this book does not fully cover the unique difficulties of abusive situations, a word of caution must be given to adoptees who have come from difficult backgrounds and who are considering a reunion.

Lisa, an adoptee we met in Chapter 4, was physically abused in her birth family before she entered her adoptive family at eight months old. When Lisa was about 16 or 17 years old, she says, her recurring nightmare of the abuse had lessened to about ten times a year.

Lisa's search for her birth mother led her first to her birth brother, Jim. When Lisa met Jim her nightmares again became more frequent. "Just meeting him, all the memories came back, if you want to call them memories," she remarks. Some clinicians and researchers believe that prenatal and infant memories exist and can replay themselves in our dreams, helping to shape our conscious and subconscious lives.

"I'm still angry," says Lisa, "but what I've been doing over the past three years is just keeping it inside. One day when I'm ready to accept it all, accept the fact that I was abused, then I'll let it all out."

It's important for adoptees from abusive homes to be aware that a reunion may trigger painful and shocking memories, which may manifest themselves as dreams, physical symptoms or actual flashbacks. The best way to cope is to seek professional help.

THE BIRTH MOTHER'S EXPERIENCE

Recapturing lost years is impossible. But recreating them by telling stories, sharing photographs and simply "being together" is a popular pastime in the first weeks and months following a reunion.

Tina felt a strong need to bond with her son, John, in the same way that she had bonded with her other children throughout their growing years.

"John would come down sick with a cold and he would

wait for me to rub Vicks on his chest — at 21 years old!" says Tina. "I loved it. I showed him how I used to care for David [Tina's later-born son] when he was little. I would write 'I love you' on his chest, and he would guess what I had written. We would play these little games. But John was 21.

"Those are the things I never got to do for him. He satisfied my maternal needs and he obviously needed to be mothered, too, or he wouldn't have allowed me to do it."

For birth mothers who live close to their children, daily contact is a common occurrence during the honeymoon stage of a reunion.

Joanne's adoptive parents lived in the same town as Rosemary, her birth mother. Joanne, however, had moved away from home to a city two hours away. When Joanne was in town, she stayed at Rosemary's. "We also exchanged letters all summer," says Rosemary.

Rosemary was concerned that Joanne's frequent visits might be threatening to Joanne's adoptive parents.

"I didn't want to cause any trouble," says Rosemary, but her daughter assured her that her adoptive parents were comfortable with the arrangements. "Later, I found out that she had lied to me. Her parents didn't even know she was in town," Rosemary shakes her head.

Wanting to "catch up" is a natural desire that is difficult to dampen. Other family members and friends, however, may feel neglected as you scramble to establish a relationship with your birth child.

One birth mother says, "I'm not a selfish person, but the first year I felt so selfish and self-centred. The mothering of my other children was not adequate."

Karen's birth daughter, Susan, lives thousands of miles away from her, and even though Karen couldn't call her every day, she comments, "I was still on cloud nine after I came home [from her reunion]. There was a strange elation and a feeling of unreality for a long time, many weeks later."

TELLING THE ADOPTEE ABOUT THE BIRTH FATHER

While two people might participate in a reunion — birth mother and adoptee — the absent birth father remains a strong presence at this meeting as well. He may not be physically present, but he is surely there in the mind of the birth mother, the adoptee, or both.

Some birth mothers choose to tell the story of the birth father before the reunion, by telephone, letter, or through a social work agency. For others, this does not happen until after the reunion.

"Joanne kept bugging me to tell her the name of her birth father," says Rosemary. Eventually, Rosemary capitulated by revealing the birth father's first name, and that satisfied her daughter for a short while.

Then Joanne started pressuring Rosemary again to tell her more about her birth father.

"I told her I still wasn't ready, and I didn't think she was ready, either. I was still bitter and very angry with him."

Some birth mothers are unable to tell their child about the birth father because they were raped, or were involved with the man only briefly and do not have a lot of information. Others were involved with more than one partner and are not sure of the birth father's identity. Or perhaps the birth mother was the victim of an incestuous relationship. These are all cases where a sensitive social worker is an invaluable support to the birth mother and to the adoptee.

If the birth mother suffered any such trauma, the reunion issues become that much more complicated. Because these situations seem to occur in a minimal number of cases, they fall outside the scope of this book. Reunitees who have to deal with such traumatic circumstances would be well advised to seek personal support through counselling, either through their social worker or an independent source.

Eventually, most reunited adoptees are able to learn about their birth fathers. It's important for adoptees to recognize that the birth mother has the right to disclose information when she is comfortable doing so, and that this may be a difficult subject for her. On the other hand, birth mothers must realize that knowledge of the birth father is their child's birthright.

TELLING THE BIRTH FATHER ABOUT THE ADOPTEE

Probably as difficult for the birth mother as telling her child about the birth father, is telling the birth father about their child. Again, it is usually the adoptee who initiates contact with the birth father.

"I had called Brian four years ago and told him that I was searching for Joanne," says Rosemary. After the reunion, she called him again. This time, she had news of her success.

"When I told Brian I'd found Joanne, he said, 'Holy cow, really? When? Where?'"

Rosemary asked Brian if he'd like to meet their daughter. According to Rosemary, he was scared, but he agreed to meet Joanne.

While Rosemary's search had provided an opportunity for mental preparation, for Brian, a reunion was more or less "out of the blue." He asked Rosemary if he could meet Rosemary first. Many birth mothers report a similar reaction from their ex-partners.

"He told me he just wanted to sit and talk to me," says Rosemary, "So we met the next day for lunch."

By this time married with four subsequent children, Rosemary recalls the anxiety caused by her reunion with Joanne's birth father.

"It ended up being a two-hour lunch. I was afraid and very

nervous. I brought the scrapbook that I'd made from the time I started looking for Joanne until the time I found her.

"Before the bill came he said, 'Boy, I really missed out, didn't I?' I thought, 'I don't want to hear this, Brian.' He's got two children at home, so now he understands. Then he said, 'Boy, you look good.' He started coming on to me. Same old thing. But this time I felt different. I didn't want anything from him.

"I'll admit it. I really did love him," says Rosemary. "And I was trying to come to terms with the whole thing. I was afraid of being alone with him again. I think up until this day I'm afraid of being alone with him, because we do have something between us: we've got Joanne. I think there'll always be an interest in somebody you've had a strong relationship with. And our relationship was good until I got pregnant with Joanne."

Karen is another birth mother who found that her ex-lover's ardour hadn't cooled over the years.

Karen wrote to Susan's birth father to tell him about Susan. He hadn't known Karen was pregnant.

"He called me right away," says Karen, "and said 'Meet me for lunch.' I said, 'That's not why I'm contacting you. Susan wants to meet you, not me.'"

ANNOUNCING THE ADOPTEE'S ARRIVAL

Announcing the arrival of a baby is one thing. Announcing the return of a fully grown adult "child" whom nobody knew existed is quite another. For birth mothers, this often means telling their subsequent offspring about their new sibling or half-sibling, a prospect that invariably instills terror into the hardiest of souls.

When my birth mother told my two brothers about me, her elder son's response dispelled her worries: "Why didn't you tell us earlier, Mom?" he asked. Both brothers wanted to meet me, and she was relieved.

Karen says her honeymoon stage was "crushed" when she decided she should tell her other children. Karen wanted Susan to be able to visit, so she decided to reveal her long-kept secret. Her three subsequent children were aged 14, 12 and 4 when the revelation occurred.

"I told the oldest one first, and she just went bananas and yelled and screamed," says Karen. "I was afraid she'd say 'My mother's a whore.' That's what I was expecting. But she never did."

Instead, Karen's 14-year-old wanted to be the first-born, wanted to have the first grandchildren and wanted to be the first in everything, says Karen. "I told my minister that I had told Lynne and she said, 'Poor Lynne, she's not the first-born. I'll bet that put her nose out of joint!' My minister knew how Lynne would react, but I wasn't prepared for it.

"I pointed out to Lynne that she was her father's and my first-born and nothing was going to change that. She still hasn't adjusted. She avoids the subject. She'll join in a conversation about Susan, but she won't initiate a conversation about her."

Karen worked to resolve this difficulty, with some success. On Susan's first visit to Karen's home, Karen arranged for Susan and Lynne to have time alone together.

"I left them alone for about an hour," says Karen, "As far as I know, they got along fine. I had the idea that Lynne imagined Susan as a horrible monster trying to take her mother away. The fact that she's just a woman, a normal, average human being, and that there's nothing to be afraid of, came across at that meeting. There were never again the sort of horrible vibes I used to get before their meeting."

Karen's two other children experienced their own unique reactions to the news of their "big sister."

Darlene, the next in line, was hoping for an older sister she'd have more in common with than the one with whom she'd grown up. Birth children have fantasies too!

"Darlene is bubbly and outgoing," says Karen, "and she was very excited and caught up in the romance of it all. 'My mother has this mysterious past. How exciting!' But that's old hat now."

While Karen's youngest daughter knows about Susan, she "doesn't really grasp the whole story," says Karen. "I think she's too young and I don't intend to fill her in for a while."

Ursula's son and daughter had very distinct reactions when told of their half-brother. Ursula says that Mark felt that she had been "bad" because she'd conceived an illegitimate child.

"My daughter, on the other hand," says Ursula, "was very happy and said, 'When am I going to meet him?'"

Rosemary's family, at the time that she contacted her birth daughter Joanne, consisted of two sons, aged 12 and 9, and a 5-year-old daughter. "It was really scary telling the other kids," admits Rosemary.

When Rosemary's elder son, Rob, first learned about his big sister, he cried and said, "'Mom, how could you ever give one of us away?'" says Rosemary. "I didn't need to hear that. But he got over it."

The next child to learn of Joanne's existence was Rosemary's other son. When she told him, he said nothing, walked out of the room and into his bedroom, sobbing. "I went into the bedroom and put my arms around him and we both cried and cried."

Later, Karen began to tell her acquaintances and friends, and says, "I've only had one, maybe two reactions that I thought were strange.

"I have one friend who was raised by a single parent. She made a few comments about placing a child for adoption, then said, 'My grandfather said my mother had made a mistake so she had to raise me.' She said it to me in such a way that she implied that I should have raised Susan as penance. But a child should not be a punishment, nor should a mother be punished," declares Karen.

After hearing from Susan for the first time, Karen was so excited that she called her friend, Renee, who was also a birth mother. Karen had known that Renee was a birth mother, but Renee was not aware that Karen knew her secret, nor that she had also relinquished her first-born.

"I told Renee about Susan and said that she had contacted me," says Karen. "I said the reason why I went away was the same reason that Renee had gone away. She nearly fell apart.

"I told Renee how I knew [about her being a birth mother]. I also told her that there was a possibility that her child might be found. She was absolutely devastated. She hasn't spoken to me since. We've written a couple of times, but her family doesn't know [about her having relinquished a child], so there's no way she can talk about it."

Karen's own birth mother and father died having never known about their granddaughter Susan's birth.

THE LIVE-IN ADOPTEE

While it's not the norm, some birth mothers do end up having their offspring live with them shortly after the reunion. This usually happens if the birth mother and/or adoptee is either chronologically or psychologically young, and/or if the adoptee has had some difficulty in her adoptive home.

Especially when the birth parents are married and living together, they may pressure a young adoptee to move in with them. Sometimes this occurs if the birth parents' marriage is unstable. The parallel to the couple who believe a new baby will save their marriage is startling. The adoptee may (unwisely) acquiesce as the fear of losing these new "parents" looms large.

It is during this "live-in" situation that the clash between an adoptee's life in the adoptive home and her new home can become most apparent. Rosemary remembers her birth daughter's "live-in" experience as disastrous for everyone.

"Joanne's living with us was the most terrible experience I've ever had," says Rosemary. "I wanted to give her some sense of responsibility, but she didn't want to take it — especially not from me."

Rosemary did everything she could to make her daughter feel at home. Her efforts backfired. "Joanne thought she didn't have to do anything around the house, that she could come and go as she pleased and not answer to anybody," says Rosemary. "I didn't like it. I thought, 'She's not a good example to my other kids.'"

Joanne's attitude caused a rift between Rosemary and her other children. "Robert, Rosemary's son, asked, 'Mom, how come Joanne doesn't have to do anything? She comes and goes as she pleases, she spends two hours in the shower, she doesn't clean up after herself; why should I have to do it?' And," comments Rosemary, "I could see his point."

Rosemary contacted the social worker who had facilitated her reunion to solicit the support she needed to assert herself with Joanne and to reinforce the family rules.

"At the end, I said to myself, 'What have I accomplished out of this? Nothing. I'm bitter towards her. I don't like her. I love her, but I don't like her."

It is during the honeymoon phase that an adoptee will often move in with her birth mother. But, as in Rosemary's case, a live-in situation rarely lasts for more than a few weeks or months. Like most other short-term issues, the fantasies and unrealistic expectations of the first few months after the reunion eventually wear off and the reunitees gain a more balanced perspective. Rosemary was wise to seek help from someone she trusted. Other birth mothers may also wish to consult a social worker, a counsellor or a trusted friend or family member to help them sort through their feelings and resolve issues arising from a live-in situation.

DEALING WITH THE ADOPTIVE PARENTS

Although in most cases the birth mother does not expect or wish the adoptee to move in with her, most birth mothers do desire a relationship with their newly recovered child. Even so, most birth mothers are sensitive towards the adoptive mother.[24] Because they are grateful to the woman who has raised their child, they are reluctant to do or say anything that might upset the relationship between the adoptive mother and the adoptee.

Tina's attitude is a healthy example of co-operation and unselfish love.

"If a mother can love two children, why can't a child love two mothers?" asks Tina. This is an ideal that may be difficult for some people to live up to.

Tina met her son's adoptive mother soon after she met John. "I looked at her and said, 'I just want you to know that I'm not here to hurt you,'" says Tina. "She just said, 'Oh, that's fine, dear.' She was really calm the whole time."

Though Karen had the rare opportunity of choosing her daughter's adoptive parents, she didn't have such an easy time making contact after the reunion. "I asked Susan if I could meet her parents and she said, 'No way.' She thought her mother wouldn't want to, but I don't think she even asked her mother to meet me. So I sent a letter to them through Susan.

"I left the letter open so that Susan could read it," says Karen. "In my letter I explained that I had chosen them and that there was no reason for them to dislike or fear me and that I had given them something that they couldn't have themselves. I said if I didn't want them to have my child, I wouldn't have given her to them in the first place.

"I told them that because I was a birth mother it didn't give me any priority, that Susan was bonded to them and that there was no way I could ever replace them even if I wanted to. You can't take 30 years out of a person's life."

Ursula's first contact with her son's adoptive mother was by telephone.

"We talked for at least half an hour," remembers Ursula. "She was very nice, and I told her over and over again that I'm not going to take the love away from her that she has with her son, that I would never do that.

"I told her that I had looked a long time to find him and she said, 'I'm glad you left it to this age. If you had done it when he was 16 or 17 years old, I don't think we could have coped.' I said 'I understand that. And I couldn't have coped if I had found him any earlier, because I was not as mature as I am now.'

"You learn something new and different every day, and I compare how I am today with how I was many years ago. When I finally did find my son, all I wanted to do was to reassure her and to thank her for raising him."

Birth mothers who meet and like their child's adoptive mother feel a new sense of peace about the adoption. Knowing that their child was raised well alleviates the years of wondering and worrying about their child. It may also reassure a birth mother that she made the best decision under the circumstances. These feelings enhance the birth mother's sense of worth.

If a birth mother is accepted and respected by her child's adoptive mother, there is less likelihood of a conflict about who is the adoptee's mother. Each will acknowledge the other's role in the adoptee's life, and harmony will prevail.

The birth mother's life may be complicated, however, as she faces the challenge of establishing her identity in connection with the adoptee. Birth mothers often feel hurt because of their offspring's confusion over how to address them.

"It's so terrible, because he still hasn't called me anything," says Ursula. "He hasn't called me mother, or Ursula. He hasn't got that sorted out. I understand. It hasn't been that long. I haven't pushed it. But I would like to talk to his girlfriend and find out how he addresses me to her."

Karen says, "At first Susan called me Karen, and I signed all my letters and telegrams 'Karen.' But now she calls me 'mom.' The first time she called me 'mom' was last year [four years after their reunion]. We were on the phone and all of a sudden she was calling me 'mom.'

"I felt very strange. I felt rather guilty about it. I mean, I liked it, but I think that if I met her parents that I'd feel a lot better."

THE ADOPTIVE PARENTS' EXPERIENCE

As mentioned earlier, the adoptive parents described in this book are, for the most part, supportive of their children's reunions. These adoptive parents almost unanimously labelled their child's curiosity about their birth parents to be "natural."

Although they viewed their child's interest in her birth family as inevitable, the reunion and the feelings that it aroused presented challenges to these adoptive parents. Louise explains her reactions after her adoptive son, Thomas, finally arrived back from his reunion: "I felt relieved that it went well. I had a lot of questions. We were curious to know what his birth mother was like, but I was afraid to ask him too much, because he's very quiet and doesn't often show his emotions. We let him tell us what went on when he was ready to."

Louise sighs deeply. "I have had such a year. There have been ups and downs. We just cautioned him at the beginning to take it easy, that he could be in for some real disappointments. Being as deep as he is, he would take it hard," says Louise.

Thomas still lives at home. Louise says, "I was scared that maybe he would leave us and we wouldn't see him. Not abandon us, but put all his energies the other way. He's not doing that. He said, 'You're still mom and dad.'

"This is a new experience for me. When he says he's going to visit his birth family for the weekend, I get a little knot in my stomach. And it always feels like a long weekend. And then he comes home and it passes.

"I said at Christmas time, 'Look at all these relatives you've got to buy for.' He said, 'No way.' Tom's birth mother sent him a Christmas card and it read, 'Love, mom.' It hurt. I thought, '*I'm* his mom.' But all in all, it's been great and we're pleased for him."

Like other adoptive parents, Louise's and Frank's worst fear for Thomas, who searched for his birth mother, was that she wouldn't want to meet him. But, contrary to this fear, says Louise, "Nobody has said, 'Why did you show up?' or, 'Why didn't you leave us alone?'" Instead, her son has developed a good relationship with his birth mother and his half-siblings, who visit occasionally at his adoptive home.

MOVING OUT

Jenny is an adoptive mother whose daughter, Claire, met her birth family when she was 20 years old.

"Claire is a very together kid, very mature for her age in a lot of ways. But I think learning that her birth parents had married had too much of an impact on Claire," said Jenny of her daughter's reunion. "I don't think she realized what was going to happen. After her reunion, I found her in a really bad mood for a couple of days."

Six months after her reunion, Claire, moved in with her birth parents.

"Claire moved to Ottawa in August, and our relationship from then on has been very, very strained. I tried to explain that I don't feel antagonistic towards her birth parents, but I'm angry about the way they're handling some things. I got really angry one time and said, 'You seem to forget that they're the ones who gave you up. Now they're just overpowering you.' Her birth father has bought her a ten-thousand-dollar electronic keyboard and all kinds of jewellery and clothes. It's just sort of like a fairytale scenario. My feeling is that my job is over. Now they've got their little girl back.

"A lot of things that happened took me by surprise. If anybody had said to me that Claire would react like this, I would have said, 'You're crazy. That's not Claire.' I don't think I'd want anybody to go through what I've been through emotionally."

Jenny attended a meeting of post-reunion adoptees and birth mothers to try to understand what her daughter Claire was feeling and how to cope with this outcome of the reunion. Nonetheless, her difficulties in her relationship with Claire continued for several years after the reunion.

Donna was also afraid that her adopted daughter, Lisa, would leave home. "Her birth mother suggested she go out west to live with her when Lisa lost her job, but Lisa wouldn't do that. She said 'I don't even know them.' This surprised me because she's never been shy about meeting people. I thought she'd jump at the chance. I wouldn't have minded, but I would have had concerns not knowing how it would turn out. Lisa still considers us her parents. She calls her mom her birth mother, so I don't really feel threatened. She knows we all love her," says Donna.

Given the choice of living a couple of thousand miles away from her adoptive family to be close to her birth family or living near her adoptive family, Lisa chose the latter. This choice may have contributed to Donna's feelings that her relationship with Lisa is better since the reunion. Donna says, "Lisa likes to talk to me about her reunion. We just seem to be more comfortable with each other. I think she's realized how much we really love her."

OFFERING AND RECEIVING SUPPORT

Louise and Frank suffered fears about their adoptive son Thomas's reunion, but from the beginning they supported his desire to search. Louise and her husband were able, in spite of their fears, to be a good support to Thomas, rather than an impediment to his reunion.

"We listened to him talk before we met them [Thomas's birth family], and it filled in a lot of gaps that we didn't know, like what were the birth parents' circumstances, and what the family was like," explains Frank.

Elaine's daughter met her birth father three years ago. "The first time she met him, we were curious to find out what he was like. Theresa was always good at telling us all about it. She always made sure she let us know what was going on. I think she tries to express that this is her home and we are her parents," says Elaine.

Fran's daughter met her birth siblings four months ago. "So far, it's been very positive, lots of excitement. The people are nice, and she has a bigger family now. I'm not saying that they'll ever be close, but she knows what her background is and she now has two brothers and a sister," says Fran.

Reunitees and their families feel both excitement and trepidation at the onset and initial unfolding of the reunion. The anxiety that accompanies the first six months or more eventually dissipates as the short-term issues are resolved. However, as adoptees, birth families and adoptive families become accustomed to each other, more complex issues begin to surface, as we'll see in the next chapter.

THINGS TO REMEMBER

Anxiety tends to magnify difficulties, both large and small, at the beginning of a reunion. Here are some things to consider in your initial struggles. Remember, the short-term issues of a reunion may well turn into shared anecdotes in the long term, as your comfort with the situation increases and your anxiety decreases.

FOR THE ADOPTEE:

(1) Don't expect your reunion to "fix" your feelings about your adoption. It won't.

(2) Keep the lines of communication open with your adoptive parents, if they're comfortable hearing about the reunion. Remember, you don't have to tell them every detail. This is *your* reunion. Just reassure them.

(3) Find someone you can talk to about your feelings, especially another reunitee. You might want to start a support group of your own.

(4) Different feelings may set in with every new birth family member that you meet. Take time to work through each reunion experience.

(5) Don't neglect your husband, wife, kids, dog or yourself. Give yourself a break.

(6) Don't get "carried away" or deceived by the honeymoon stage. Remember, it takes time to get to know other people, including birth family members.

FOR THE BIRTH MOTHER:

(1) Remember you can never recapture the past, but you do have a future.

(2) Pace yourself. Try not to overwhelm the adoptee with too many calls or visits.

(3) Even though he may sympathize, don't expect your husband to fully understand your feelings. Find someone who does and who is willing to listen.

(4) Don't neglect your husband, wife, kids, dog or yourself. Give yourself a break.

FOR THE ADOPTIVE PARENTS:

(1) If your adopted child isn't sharing her reunion experience with you, she may be afraid of hurting your feelings. Remember that this is not a sign of rejection; it may be a sign of love and respect.

(2) If you want to know how the reunion's going, ask. But don't pry.

(3) Congratulate yourself for your courage in supporting your son or daughter's reunion.

FOR ALL:

(1) Enjoy the initial relief and euphoria of a good reunion. But prepare yourself for the possibility of difficult times ahead.

(2) Don't expect problems, but make sure you've got support if they do materialize.

§

CHAPTER 10

POST REUNION: LONG-TERM ISSUES

My birth mother and I now write only occasionally. Once in a while, we call each other on the phone. But when we get together, we hug each other and I am glad she had the generosity of spirit to meet me after so many years. And, just as important, she has continued to accept me in her life, even though I may not be the daughter she had imagined.

— *M. M.*

UNTIL THREE YEARS after my reunion with my birth mother, I believed I had uncovered and resolved all the emotions, conflicts and expectations connected with my adoption and reunion. Then one afternoon, very suddenly, there sprang up a flood of emotions and memories that seemed to emanate from my subconscious. As I write these words, my reunion is nearly five years old, and I'm still discovering new feelings and experiencing challenges related to my reunion. I've come to believe, along with others in the field, that adoption is literally a life-long process and so, too, is the aftermath of a reunion. Reunions only partially heal past wounds. They can, at least temporarily, deepen others. A sense of loss can be magnified if, as in my case, you meet people you love and feel a connection with.

Some long-term issues may never be completely resolved. For example, an adoptee may to some degree continue to feel angry that she was denied the right to know her birth mother as she grew up. A birth mother may never recover from the pain of separation and the loss of enjoying her child's infancy and youth, even though she has met her son or daughter in adulthood.

While short-term issues tend to be more practical in nature — such as how to address your counterpart or with whom to spend Christmas vacation — many long-term difficulties tend to evolve from deep and complex emotions that must be identified, understood and resolved, if possible.

Each reunitee has to make her own decision whether or not to share her negative feelings with her counterpart. As a guide, remember that the psychological toll of repression has already been high for adoptees, birth mothers and adoptive families. Instead of denying painful issues, one may wish to consider seeing a counsellor to help work through one's feelings. By this stage in the reunion, most reunitees have already discovered that if they don't attend to problems as they develop, these problems will come back to haunt them later.

By "long-term" issues I am referring to challenges besetting a reunion that is typically at least six months old. Many of these issues may not arise until a year or more after the actual reunion.

THE ADOPTEE'S EXPERIENCE

It may take a long time, but eventually adoptees may begin to feel like family members in their birth family, instead of like acquaintances or friends. Gord, an adoptee, says, "A lot happened in the first year of our reunion. I called my birth mother 'Vicky.' We became friends. We had a lot of intense conversations about what had happened to her. She told me everything, even that I was conceived in the back seat of a car.

"We are still really interested in each other. I feel more of a bond with her now; she's a part of my life. It's progressed to where we feel like family." As the bond between reunitees deepens, interpersonal conflicts will probably develop, as they do in all families.

MAINTAINING THE CONNECTION

An important and ongoing long-term issue is how much contact to maintain with one's counterpart. A clash of expectations is often at the heart of this question. It's difficult to know what the other person wants, and even more difficult to live up to someone else's expectations, especially when you're not sure what those expectations are and you're too afraid to ask!

"At first I thought it was fine and dandy to see Vicky twice a week. But later I'd get annoyed when she'd call and say, 'So-and-so's in town, it would be nice if you could stop by,' or, 'What are you doing after work tonight?' I hate demands on my life. I felt overwhelmed for a while, as if there were too many people in my life already, but then I went digging for more. Even a year after we met we were still calling each other every day," says Gord.

After I met my own birth mother, I felt obligated to call her regularly. I don't do that with my adoptive family, and I didn't want to do it with my birth mother. But I was afraid of losing her again. Sometimes I worried that she was hurt because I didn't call or write as much as she would have liked. I was afraid that I wasn't the kind of daughter she would have raised or that she wanted.

Part of what I was feeling was "adoptee insecurity," a left-over of feeling insecure as I grew up. Just as adoptive parents say they are always afraid they'll lose the adoptee, the adoptee has a constant fear that she'll lose her birth family again. I now realize I expected my reunion to "fix" everything. It didn't.

Many adoptees feel that they aren't living up to what's expected of them. On the other hand, adoptees can also feel let down by a lack of contact.

Realizing that lack of contact is not rejection is a crucial step. Adoptees are particularly sensitive to feelings of rejection or abandonment, and must remind themselves that their birth family may be just as busy as they are. This doesn't necessarily mean that they aren't important to their birth mother. It's important to try not to second-guess your counterpart, and to give the benefit of the doubt rather than to sink into depression and fantasies of being rebuffed.

It's just as important to respect the wishes of others, and, while taking care of your own needs, to make sure that you're not invading someone else's privacy with too many telephone calls or unwanted visits. Striking a balance through communication and sensitivity is the key to resolving this dilemma. Ask your birth family members what they want. And remember that their needs will probably fluctuate over time, just as your needs will. As the reunion progresses, it's a good idea to "check in" on a regular basis to determine your place in your birth mother's life at any given time.

As my reunion has unfolded, my birth mother and I have called each other less often and we rarely write letters. But we are so much alike and we both work such long hours that our twice-monthly or monthly telephone calls are appropriate for us. We laugh when we exchange stories of our busy schedules and acknowledge that we would like to spend more time together but that it's impractical.

RECLAIMING YOUR IDENTITY

One of the most commonly reported long-term benefits of reunions is that adoptees develop a stronger sense of identity. One 29-year-old adoptee wrote to me just after meeting her birth mother: "I have never felt so complete as a person."

Physical mirroring is a powerful way for adoptees to realize and internalize their place in a genetic lineage. Adoptees commonly state that, through their reunion, they hope to find someone who looks like them. Outward resemblance to other human beings says to the world "we belong together" in a way that words can't. It's something birth families take for granted. Physical similarities can help cement psychological bonding. It has been said that people tend to feel more at ease with others who look like they do.[25]

For the adoptee who is looking for personality and physical similarities in her birth mother and who doesn't find them, meeting her extended family may be the solution. Many birth mothers have said, "When we met, I thought you looked more like your birth father than me," or, "like aunt Ellen," "like your great-grandmother," etc.

While finding someone who looks like you is an indescribable thrill for an adoptee, most do not realize that they may also meet someone who tells the same corny jokes — or who hates the same foods!

Three years after meeting my birth mother, we took a trip to Germany to meet my extended birth family. I met a first-cousin-once-removed (an apt title!) in Hanover and within ten minutes we were saying the same thing at the same time. I immediately felt a kinship with her that had no parallel in my adoptive family.

Reclaiming your identity sometimes means embracing a culture and a nationality that are foreign to your adoptive family. After my original trek to Germany to meet my relatives, I returned to visit, again, this special relative. On the flight over, I was shocked by the thoughts and feelings that suddenly assailed me as I looked out the tiny window to the terrain below.

"This is my homeland," I thought, as I gazed at the strips of green fields stretching below me. It was a bizarre and unexpected notion, but I felt it in my bones. For the first time in my life, I felt a sense of ancestry. I imagined my birth parents, grandparents and forbears living on this land. As the sun streamed through the window, I imagined the sunshine on their backs as they planted their gardens. I imagined their children going to school, and I felt connected with the chain of blood relatives, past and present, born in this country. It was incredible. I finally felt that I understood my adoptive family's fascination with their Scottish genealogy and the many stories and anecdotes that make up their uniquely woven family tapestry. Now I, too, was rooted in history.

BIRTH FATHER ISSUES

There are two halves to the adoptee's history — maternal and paternal. There may be special issues ahead for the adoptee who later pursues her paternal family after she has forged a link with her maternal family.

One adoptee recalls hearing two entirely different stories from her birth mother and her birth father about their relationship. While her birth mother felt her relationship with the birth father was a "great romance," the birth father told his daughter that he had never been serious about the birth mother. The now 30-year-old adoptee decided not to share this information with her birth mother, but knowledge of her birth father's contradictory perceptions was awkward for her — one more family secret to guard.

For some, adoption occurred because their teenage parents

were not allowed to marry. When relationships that had been happy and healthy ended prematurely due to family pressure, there are powerful unresolved feelings on the part of both birth parents.

Angela's birth parents separated after the pregnancy was discovered due to pressure from her birth mother's father, who refused to allow the two to marry as planned. After Angela had met both birth parents, her birth mother asked for her birth father's telephone number.

"I panicked," says Angela. "Part of me was glad, because I felt they had been thinking about each other all these years. But part of me was terrified, because they were both married to other people. What if they had an affair?"

Angela was worried about "being in the middle" and being blamed if her birth parents started a relationship again after all those years.

"My worst fear," says Angela, "was that I would lose my half-siblings." Angela worried that if her half-brothers, aged 9, 11 and 13, saw less of their mother, or if her mother's marriage split up, it would be her fault because she was the one who had instigated the reunion. The old pattern of guilt persisted.

Although the idea of her birth parents reuniting might please or upset an adoptee, the prospect of a meeting with both birth parents may be hard for the adoptee to resist. The adoptee may feel that she has a "right" to spend time with both birth parents. This meeting, however, might not elicit approval from everyone it affects. The birth parents' spouses, children and friends should be considered. It's difficult to explain the adoptee's needs for a "family" get-together to those who haven't been adopted, but the analogy of a completed puzzle is an apt one. It's not as satisfying when one piece is missing, compared to having the whole picture there in front of you to gaze at, to touch.

As one birth father said, "We're family." Even though he,

the birth mother and their daughter had been apart for 30 years, he felt that the bond would never break.

APPRECIATING YOUR ADOPTIVE PARENTS

In spite of their new relationship with their birth mother, or perhaps because of it, many adoptees reaffirm their relationship with their adoptive parents after their reunion. The majority of adoptees report that their relationship with their adoptive parents has improved or stayed the same, compared to before the reunion.

Gord says of his adoptive parents, "I always knew who my parents were, but my reunion has reaffirmed that and brought us closer together and allowed me to appreciate them.

"My whole life I thought, 'Geez, I live in the suburbs, we've got a two-car garage, I have a cat, a dog, a cottage...I've always rebelled against these things. My reunion made me go back and say, 'Wow! I live in the suburbs, I've got a cat, a dog; my parents have a cottage.' It made me sit back and realize that I have it really good. It's made me open to caring for them more.

"Probably for the first time in my life I sat back and thought, 'Yeah, these are my parents.' I wouldn't want anything else."

One adoptee, whose birth mother passed away shortly after they met, says, "In visiting her and in actively arranging for her funeral, I learned a great deal about people, life and myself. I was never, in all my life, as grateful to my adoptive family for the life they had given me as I was that day. And I was also grateful to my birth mother who, by letting me go, gave us all a better life."[26]

COMBINING FAMILIES AND
MEETING NEW FAMILY MEMBERS

The decision to incorporate your birth family into your adoptive family is a complex one. Even more complex is how to do so. For many reunitees, this meeting does not take place until a year or several years after the reunion. But for some, it may occur within the first year of a reunion.

Gord's adoptive parents met his birth mother about a year after his reunion. For Gord, as for most adoptees, contact between his birth mother and his adoptive family has remained cordial, but minimal.

"Mom wanted to have Vicky over at Christmas time," says Gord. "Vicky was terrified of meeting my parents and they were just as terrified as she was. But they were meeting her on their own turf, which was the best way for them to do it.

"I got the impression that my parents were praying the whole time that nobody would come to the door while my birth mother was visiting. They didn't want to have to explain who she was. At that point they hadn't told anyone about my reunion.

"Vicky was there for two or three hours, and after a while everyone started to unwind and feel comfortable with each other."

Although Gord had told his adoptive parents about his reunion, he hadn't told his adoptive grandparents, who were at his home when his birth mother arrived. While adoptees are sometimes successful in letting go of "protecting" their adoptive parents from their reunion, many continue to feel that their adoptive grandparents, because of their age, may never understand their need for a reunion. An adoptee may feel compelled to uphold an uncomfortable double standard, sharing news of her birth mother with adoptive parents, but not with adoptive grandparents. Unfortunately, this situation only creates more secrets. It also circumvents the possibility of the adoptive grandparents accepting the reunion. In the long run, it may be healthier for an adoptee to maintain honesty about her reunion rather than to hide it from adoptive family members.

In my own case, my adoptive father met my birth mother the same day I did. We have had the occasional evenings out since then, and Christmas and birthday cards are shared between my adoptive father and my birth mother.

Two years after my reunion with my birth mother, I met my birth father. Later my adoptive dad, on his own initiative, invited my birth father to dinner alone. Afterwards, he told me that their meeting had gone well and he felt that they had liked and "understood" each other. This was their only meeting, and it's a rare occurrence in the history of post-adoption reunions. Having my dad show so much interest and caring has sustained me through the many twists and turns of post-reunion life.

While adoptees may be successful in establishing a relationship with birth parents, extended birth relatives may not be as enthusiastic.

One adoptee whose reunion is three years old says, "I've met my birth mother, her parents and her brother, but her sister refuses to have anything to do with me. It hurts, but not nearly as much as it did at first."

This kind of "rejection," while not as devastating as being rejected by a birth parent, still holds a sting for the adoptee. Relatives may fear "reliving" the past or may hold antiquated prejudices towards "illegitimate" children. Or maybe they're simply too busy or distracted. They may not realize how important they are to the adoptee who is trying to reconnect with her birth family, because they grew up with their own birth family. Whatever the reason, their refusal to meet the adoptee may feed the adoptee's feelings of rejection and low self-esteem. A feeling of helplessness is also reinforced. The adoptee was helpless when her fate to be adopted was decided, and she remains helpless when she feels that she cannot approach a relative who refuses to accept her.

"I felt invisible," says the 28-year-old adoptee whose birth aunt would not meet her. "She won't even talk about me. It's like I don't even exist. Yet I've seen many pictures of her, and heard about her life from my birth mother. It's like I have a vicarious relationship with my aunt through my birth mother."

When adoptees feel slighted or rejected by birth family members, family support from a husband, children and adoptive parents can help. These family members can emphasize the love they feel for the adoptee and help her to maintain a healthy perspective. They can also reassure her that although she may feel rejected now, people change and there is always hope for the future.

RELEASING ANGER AND DEPRESSION

The most difficult and overwhelming long-term post-reunion issue is confronting feelings of anger, depression and sadness that have ripened with the realization that what has been lost will never be fully recovered.

After a reunion, these feelings are hooked up with their origins, and the result is extremely painful. For some adoptees, their anguish is first expressed at the onset of a reunion. During my first weekend visit at my birth mother's home shortly after we'd met, she and I stayed up until three o'clock in the morning. I cried and told her that, yes, I had felt that I had been rejected. I thought that this sharing meant that I was in touch with my feelings. I was shocked when their full intensity hit me three years later, after this initial release.

As I grew up, my anger focussed mainly on my birth grandfather, who had given my birth mother the choice of giving up her family or me. Three years after my reunion, I wrote

him a long letter. As I wrote, a rage, the intensity of which surprised me, came pouring onto the pages. I asked him if he'd
thought about what would happen to me after my mother gave
me up? Did he ever think about me, did he know what being
adopted was like? What had given him the right to decide my
fate? Why did he think I needed my family less than he needed
his? I cried; I vented anger and pain. Later, I chose not to
share this letter with him. He was 87 years old, and I felt
relieved by the process of writing — the anger towards him
had dissipated to the point where it was almost gone.

Sometimes the universe has to hit us over the head to tell
us something. For me, it took having a reunion with nearly
every living birth relative, working in adoption disclosure at a
Children's Aid Society for a year-and-a-half, and researching
and writing this book for five years, before I finally tapped into
my repressed emotions. I had been transcribing notes from an
adoption reunion conference and I had typed a remark made
by one of the lecturers: "Adoptees are terminally sad." This
sentence hit me like a shock wave and I began to sob. The next
three days revealed many repressed emotions.

Am I slow? I don't think so. I think that adoptees of closed
adoptions are so fully versed in what's expected of them, it can
take this kind of "multiple-shock treatment" to shatter the
thick layers of denial built in to the closed adoption system.

And the lessons keep coming. Five years after my reunion
with my birth mother, I attended a family reunion with my
adoptive family. My sister and cousin sat poring over the family genealogy to find out if our generation had been included in
the most recent publication. I became wistful and left the
room. I *knew* that my lineage would not be found on those
pages. I'd been edited out of my own genetic line long ago.

The next day, my adoptive father, birth mother and I par-
ticipated in a photo/interview session together at my birth
mother's home. As I sat looking at my birth mother and my

adoptive father, I was reminded that I had never felt like a full-fledged member of my adoptive family, and I now realized that I would also never completely belong to my birth mother's family. I was not raised by them, I had never fought with my half-brothers as a child, I wasn't around when they were born, and I would never recapture the years of childhood with its treasury of memories or share in their relationships with their extended family and friends. Suddenly, as I sat between my birth mother and my adoptive father, I realized that I would always feel just that — isolated somewhere between families, belonging to both and to neither at the same time.

THE BIRTH MOTHER'S EXPERIENCE

As with any other life-changing experience, there are both positive and negative outcomes of a post-adoption reunion. Among the positives are the increased levels of self-esteem and self-acceptance reported by many birth mothers. Often, a stigma has been lifted; they feel more complete, confident and at peace with themselves. They partially or totally overcome the traumas caused by the relinquishment of their (usually) first-born children.

"She's getting stronger and I am too," says Karen of herself and her birth daughter, Susan.

"Since I've met her, my self-image has just kept improving and improving. Before my reunion, I felt that I was an unwed mother and that's the way I always saw myself. I think that's probably one of the reasons that I had a lot of trouble in my marriage. I put my husband on a pedestal because he married me, in spite of the fact that I was an unwed mother.

"Before I met Susan, I was very closed about my life. That's changed. Now I don't care who knows," says Karen, who developed agoraphobia, rarely leaving her basement apartment for a year. Since her reunion, she's completely recovered.

While the reunion holds rewards for birth mothers, problems may exist in the relationship between a birth mother and an adoptee even years after a reunion. Some of the difficulties stem from the intense desire to bond with a virtual stranger.

"I've seen Stephen four times now in two years," says Ursula. "I talk too much, and I hate myself for it. He's very quiet, and when he says something, he doesn't say a lot. Then there is this silence and I think, 'Oh my God, somebody has to talk.' He is my son, but we are still strangers and I have to remember that."

Tina remembers her struggle to define her relationship with her son, John. This was particularly challenging since John had been in trouble with the law and had difficult family relationships. Tina wrestled with her urge to step in to nurture and to educate John.

Tina says, "When I first met John, I said to him, 'I want you to know that no matter what you've ever done, or what you ever do, from now on, no matter how bad it is, we'll work it out,' and I meant it. He said he feels the same way about me.

"Every little thing that happens, bad or good," says Tina, "is a bonding. We're still working on bonding."

Sometimes the adoptee and the birth mother hold different expectations as to the birth mother's role. This clash in role definition can be difficult for the birth mother to cope with.

"I think she would like me to be her housekeeper," says Karen of Susan, her birth daughter. "Susan wants the 'motherly' mother, kind of bustling around the kitchen waiting on her. She wants me to be a homebody, making pies and cookies. And that's not the kind of mother I am."

Tina also had difficulties fulfilling her son's expectations of what a "mother" is.

"John's adoptive mother catered to him, but I'm not Suzy Homemaker. I don't cook because I don't enjoy it. I said to John, 'I don't expect to be endeared to you because of my cooking.' "

SO FAR AWAY

Birth mothers who live far away from their birth children lament the geographical distance. It's more difficult to establish a close relationship if this impediment is added to all the other challenges that accompany a reunion.

Ursula says, "I really hope that things are going to be even better. The trouble is the distance. It's a three-hour drive from our place to his."

Tina's son John also lived three hours away when they met. Tina wanted to play a "mothering" role after she had located John, but found this difficult because of the distance.

"I said to John, 'I'm not close enough to always pick my timing. When I see you, there are many little things I need to say.' Sometimes I tend to lecture," says Tina. Ultimately, she says, "I would like John to come and live with us. I want him to lean on us more." Tina and Roger, John's birth father, have offered to pay for further education for John. "I think if he lived with us, he would have the confidence to go back to school," says Tina.

Tina's distance problem worsened when her husband was transferred to a job in a city even farther away than when she first met John.

"I told John I was going to send him 'nag videos,'" says Tina: "'Hi, John, this is your mother. You can fast-forward this and make me look really good.'"

Distance has constrained Ursula from contacting her birth son more frequently.

"I have been very careful not to go to his city. I'm standing back and letting him do the work. I have sent cards once in a while, and sometimes he calls me."

Karen, whose birth daughter lives in a different province, worries about the cost of Susan calling her long distance. "When she hasn't called for a while, I have to keep telling myself that her husband would probably have a heart attack if she phoned, but if I feel too much time has passed and she hasn't called, I call her."

Ironically, distance can also work as a positive factor in a reunion.

"We live so far apart," says Karen, "what kind of serious problem can we have, except for atrocious phone bills? I feel isolated, but there's nothing I can do about it.

"I wouldn't say that our relationship is great. There are lots of things that still need to be worked out. But we're so far apart I don't think there's any way it'll ever change. It might be different if we were living where we could get together more often." Even so, says Karen, now that her reunion is four years old, "We're trying to build a relationship between us — a friendship and a trust. We're working towards something rather than concentrating on what we missed."

THE ABUSIVE ADOPTIVE HOME

Coming to terms with an adoptee's placement in an abusive or otherwise dysfunctional home is a heartbreaking process for birth mothers. Under the best of circumstances, it is impossible to be sure of a successful placement, particularly since, once an adoption is legally finalized by the courts, there is no further intervention or follow-up on the part of the social agency.

Sylvia laments the results of her son's adoptive upbringing, and David himself says he feels a lack of confidence because his brother was favoured, while he was punished physically by his adoptive father.

Sylvia married David's birth father, Bob, shortly after David was relinquished. "He needs a father's guidance," says Sylvia. "Bob's words and thoughts are going to have more bearing on David's way of thinking. He needs Bob more than he needs me. He needs to be given confidence in himself."

Still, Sylvia feels David's adoptive parents did their best. "They both love him. But there are times when I've wanted to say, 'You're right, David, drop 'em, you've got us. You don't need them anymore."

"But I put myself in the adoptive mother's place. She raised this child, changed his diapers, she walked the floor when he teethed, she worried about him, she was more of a mother to him than I have been or have been able to be. I'm not going to take that away from her," says Sylvia. "I look at Matthew [Sylvia's next eldest son] and think, 'What if Matthew were adopted? I wouldn't treat him any differently.' If Bob hit and abused Matthew, do you think I'd stay there? I'd put my body between the two of them. Bob wouldn't scare me.

"If I wasn't a parent myself," says Sylvia, "I probably wouldn't have understood her side of it. But I always try to put myself in her place."

Although an adoptee may have been mistreated while growing up, birth mothers must remember that they made the best decision available to them and they did their best at the time of the adoption. Their reunion is with an adult and it's important for the birth mother to grieve the loss of her parenting role but not to blame herself if the adoptee was raised poorly.

TWO MOTHERS

In a case where the adoptee has been unhappy in the adoptive home, or the adoptive home was abusive, birth mothers feel, sometimes with good reason, that there is still a lot of "mothering" to do. The desire to reparent an adoptee can cause friction between the birth mother and the adoptive mother.

"I said to David once, 'I have this little fantasy that I've always had you. I don't like having to share you, but I don't have any choice. It's a fact of life.' David's adoptive mother doesn't look at it that way," says Sylvia. "I mean, David's here because I'm here. If I weren't here, or had decided to abort, she wouldn't have had him to raise and enjoy."

Sylvia's initial meeting with David's adoptive mother occurred at a dinner with David present. Sylvia feels that this meeting went well, but the next contact with David's adoptive mother, in a telephone conversation, resulted in a dramatic turnaround.

Sylvia had arranged a party for David. She called David's adoptive mother to invite her to the celebration.

"She started to make an excuse," says Sylvia, "Then she said, 'I've been thinking about it since I met you, and I don't like sharing my son.' My mouth dropped open and my face went white."

Sylvia feels that the adoptive mother was afraid of being judged by her son's birth family. Sylvia says, "No matter what she says or how she feels, David is still my son and that's never going to change. I would just love to say to her, 'Whose son?' But David would end up being in the middle. He'd end up being hurt."

Sylvia's reluctance to defend her position as David's birth mother is understandable, given the attitude towards birth mothers at the time of David's birth. Birth mothers of the past, as we have seen, were routinely given short shrift throughout the adoption process. It's no wonder that, 21 years later, Sylvia's feelings of helplessness in relation to David have resurfaced.

Some birth mothers also find it difficult to be treated differently than adoptive mothers, another situation over which the birth mother has no control.

"He waits on her hand and foot," says Sylvia. "But he doesn't treat me like that, and it hurts. When she's around he doesn't call me mom. I anticipated that and said to him, 'When your mom's around, call her mom. That's appropriate, when there are two of us standing there.' But he doesn't call me any-thing. He finds it difficult to call me Sylvia."

Like most other birth parents, Sylvia and Bob, David's birth father, are much younger than David's adoptive parents. "He thinks it's just a riot that we're so young, Bob and I. He's enjoying the fact that we can do things with him. We can wres-tle on the floor, we can joke around, somebody farts and we all think it's funny," says Sylvia.

While the adoptee who meets a young birth parent may enjoy the experience, the age difference can cause trauma for the birth mother when the time comes to meet the adoptive mother.

"I was so emotional about meeting her," says Sylvia. "This woman was old enough to be my mother. In fact, she was the same age as my mother, 64. I was always taught to respect my elders. And this is the woman who raised my child. I was very emotional and I got diarrhea before I met her."

Regardless of the difficulties, the meeting between mothers can be a positive experience for both.

"I thanked Stephen's adoptive mother for bringing up such a beautiful boy and for the good job they did," says Ursula. "She said, 'You gave him the genes, we gave him the environ-ment.'"

AMENDING YOUR WILL

A practical consideration that arises after the reunion is whether or not to amend one's will. While the adoptee legally remains the child of the adoptive parents, some birth mothers feel that once they have been reunited, they have revived their responsibility towards their child. Others want the adoptee to feel that he or she is accepted as a full member of the family.

"I would like John to be included in my will," says Tina. "But do I divide his inheritance equally with my other son? In

Roger's mind, John's got to prove something first."

Even birth grandparents can get involved. One birth mother's father asked her, a year after her reunion, if he should include the adoptee in his will or not.

Including the adoptee in one's will may cause friction between the birth mother and her spouse, and jealousy and hurt feelings among her subsequent children. Also, the status and importance of money may be different to the adoptee than to the birth family. It's wise to try to learn the adoptive family's attitude towards financial matters before making a decision that might be misconstrued by your newly found "heir."

As reunions become the norm, perhaps future laws and/or social practice will take this dilemma into account. This would guide the birth mother who isn't sure of the most judicious way of handling the situation. For the time being, birth mothers should proceed with caution, caring and a good lawyer.

MAINTAINING THE CONNECTION

Birth mothers and their birth sons and daughters must work slowly towards a relationship that is comfortable and rewarding for both. As we have seen, being reunited after a closed adoption presents unique hurdles to relationship-building. Birth mothers must accept their current role in the adoptee's life while balancing past hurts with dreams for the future.

Like adoptees, birth mothers must negotiate the various stages of their reunion and gauge how much or how little contact would be appropriate at any given time. Ursula's relationship has changed over the four years that she's known her birth son.

"I called in the beginning a lot more than I do now," says Ursula. "We say at Parent Finders that after a while, you have to take a little step backwards. Otherwise you can be much too forceful. I send cards and phone him once in a while, and he calls me occasionally. If I go down to his home town, I'll call his [adoptive] mother and ask her if she'd like to get together for a coffee."

Karen, now three years post-reunion, would like Susan, who searched for her, to phone more often. "After all," says Karen, "she's the one who made the approach in the first place." In addition to this common complaint, Karen is never sure exactly what Susan wants. "Sometimes I think I'm calling too often and I'd better not call for a while. I don't want to impose. I'll wait about three weeks and then I can't stand it any longer and I'll call and she'll say, 'Oh, I'm so glad you called — this has gone wrong and that has gone wrong,' and then I think, 'I should have called sooner. I'm neglecting her.'"

Karen's and Susan's relationship is not as warm as Karen would like, and it is different from Karen's relationship with her other children. She's much more straightforward with the children she raised, says Karen. If one of her other children hadn't called in a while, she says, "I'd say, 'What's wrong with you? You haven't called for three days!' But I wouldn't say that to Susan."

Karen's different responses to Susan and her other children could be explained by the fact that when families grow up together, they feel that they "belong" to each other, come hell or high water. We feel more free to be ourselves because the familial bond is, in some respects, unbreakable. Having grown up together, we also know what each other's expectations are. In a reunion, however, the relationship is not only new, but much more tentative and fragile because of the vulnerability of the reunitees and a lack of precedent for their roles in each other's lives. As a result, reunitees feel that they are walking on eggshells for a long time after their reunion. Some birth mothers and adoptees never overcome this feeling.

THE ADOPTIVE PARENTS' EXPERIENCE

When adoptive parents are supportive of their son's or daughter's reunion, not only will their own family relationship deepen, but the family circle itself may expand to include birth family members.

Gerry, a 74-year-old adoptive father, was pleased about the relationship that developed between Theresa and her birth father, Bert, and he was glad that he could share in the relationship. "Right away Bert and I were established," says Gerry. "We were friends, quickly and solidly. I found that we got along perfectly together. I was really delighted to know him. I think we both shared something, Theresa being the common denominator. For Bert to feel that his little girl was loved and wanted, I think, was important. For us, if it hadn't been for Bert and Theresa's birth mother, obviously, we could have never had Theresa.

"At my birthday Bert signed a card, 'Father number Two,' and I assured him that he was just as much 'One' as I could be. And he was — I felt that. Bert and I were very close." Unfortunately, Bert died sometime later.

Frank and Louise have also met their son's birth family members — a half-brother, a half-sister, his birth mother, and his birth father's family. Louise and Frank met Thomas's birth mother first, during a visit in their own home. "I really felt sorry for her, coming in to strange people. I was on my own territory, but she was very shy," says Louise. "I can see where Thomas gets his quietness. His birth mother has been here a couple of times and she is also a shy person.

"His brother's been here a couple of times for the weekend, and Thomas is tickled to death that he's got a brother. [Thomas's only sibling while growing up was an adoptive sister.] The first thing he said to Thomas was, 'Can I call you my brother?'

"Thomas goes down there quite often, his [birth] sister has been here just briefly, and Thomas has a niece — she's been here too.

"In August, all of us went to a family reunion on his birth father's side. They invited our [adopted] daughter, but she works and couldn't go. They were just super. They organized a picnic and a barbecue, and we were included as family. They invited us to come again."

I met my own birth mother in August 1989, and the next summer my adoptive father suggested that I invite her, her husband and my two brothers to our family reunion the next summer. They came along, and my extended adoptive family enjoyed meeting them. Gatherings between birth families and adoptive families are rare, but they tend to go well as their very occurrence indicates a willingness to get along, and an open-mindedness, on the part of both families. Perhaps it's because the two families have been kept separate for so many years, through the practice of closed adoption, that a closer bond does not usually develop.

THE FEELING OF LOSING A CHILD

When the relationship between the adoptive parents and the birth parents is strained or even antagonistic, a reunion can cause on-going difficulties. For Jenny, whose daughter Claire moved in with her birth mother and father, long-term issues continue to be painful.

Jenny says, "I could have told you six months ago she'd move in with her birth family. I had an intuitive feeling. I'm very psychic. She gets along with them really well, and that part doesn't bother me. I try to put myself in their position and imagine how I'd feel if I had given a kid up and all of a sudden, 20 years later, I found her. But I would have consideration for the other person that's done all the work. I feel really hurt. I've shed a lot of tears lately." Jenny began to attend Parent Finders meetings to help her sort through her feelings.

"It's been good for me to go and hear why adoptees want to find their parents. I'm understanding that desire a lot better. I talk to my friends and I've got a good psychologist who says, 'Let it go.' I feel the one I need to talk to the most is Claire, my daughter. But she doesn't call. After my last phone call to her, I decided that was the last time I would call her."

REASSURANCES

Jenny's situation is, fortunately, a rare one, as we saw earlier in this chapter. Most adoptive parents gain their child's reassurances that they are still "mom and dad," regardless of, and sometimes even more so because of, the reunion with the birth family.

Gerry says, "I think that the relationship that Theresa had with Bert was definitely something that she would never want to miss, and neither Elaine nor I would have wanted her to miss it.

"The happiness that was engendered by the meeting with Bert was worth so much to all of us. It meant that Theresa's life was helped in so many different ways. Her general reaction, the anticipation of meeting Bert, for example, was strong, which would certainly indicate that it was of great importance to her. The fact that Theresa and her husband made several trips down there, and Bert made several trips this way, indicated a strong bond, which I think is a wonderful thing. I think that maybe Theresa and I are closer with each other as a result of that. Theresa knows that Bert was important to me and with his being important to her, the three of us were drawn together."

Although positive relationships may result from reunions,

reunions don't "fix" anything. For adoptees, they do answer questions and provide an opportunity for the adoptee to feel like a "whole" person. They allow the adoptee to claim her genetic lineage, thereby achieving a context for her life and deeper insights into her own personality. Many adoptees say that it was only after their reunion that they felt that they could move on in their lives. A reunion is therefore both an ending — to searching and wondering about the birth family — and the beginning of a new life.

For birth mothers, reunions complete a family and may extend it through a relationship with the adoptive family. Reunions put an end to worry and guilt, as the birth mother learns the outcome of her decision to place her child for adoption. The reunion allows the birth mother to move on, having come full circle with her past.

Through a reunion, adoptive parents also have the opportunity to resolve their feelings about the adoption and to gain reassurance about their own role as parents. Supporting their adoptive child through her reunion is one of the greatest gifts an adoptive parent can offer.

THINGS TO REMEMBER

FOR THE ADOPTEE:

(1) It's okay not to have constant contact after a reunion. It doesn't mean you've been abandoned or rejected. It probably means the opposite: you've been accepted as part of your birth mother's family.

(2) You are not obligated to stay in a relationship that is not healthy, whether or not you did the searching. Try to get counselling if you feel you must end the relationship.

(3) Your birth mother might never be able to give you all the answers you want, even in the long term. Don't push her into something she's not ready to deal with or to remember.

(4) It takes time to build a relationship.

FOR THE BIRTH MOTHER:

(1) It's normal for contact to have slowed down by the long-term stage. It's not an indication that your son or daughter has lost interest in you.

(2) If you can't find a support group, books such as *The Other Mother*, by birth mother Carole Schaefer, and *Birthbond: Reunions Between Birthparents and Adoptees — What Happens After*, co-written by birth mother Linda Brown and researcher Judith Gediman, might help.

FOR THE ADOPTIVE PARENTS:

(1) Your anxieties will probably be alleviated in the long-term stage.

(2) If you need support, a social worker at a Children's Aid Society can talk to you about your post-reunion feelings.

(3) You might have an extended family in the long term. Try to adjust.

(4) It's important for the adoptee to feel you accept her birth family.

FOR ALL:

(1) Reunions provide healing. With courage, love and compassion, there are long-term gains for everybody.

§

PART THREE

In Support
of Reunions

CHAPTER 11

SUPPORT AND EDUCATION

*Only after my reunion did I realize that I had taken a leap
into the unknown. I was shocked by some of my own reactions. If I hadn't belonged to a support group comprising
other reunitees, I don't know if my reunion would have survived the first two years — or if I would have survived the
first two years. The group provided the context I needed to
help me understand what I was experiencing. It was a relief
to be able to sit and cry with people who understood and
accepted me. The fact that they were not a part of my
reunion created an objectivity and a "safety net." It was
important for me to hear the birth mothers' perspectives
without having to approach my own birth mother. That was
still too scary.*

—*M. M.*

STRUGGLING AGAINST THE CURRENT of antiquated adoption
mythologies, thousands of adoptees and birth family members seeking reunion often believe they are alone. The fear
of ostracism and of dealing with painful emotions has kept
them from sharing both their status as adoptees and birth
mothers, and their reunion experiences with one another. One

33-year-old adoptee claimed she had never *met* another adoptee! Social taboos tied in to past adoption practices have stymied attempts to establish dialogue about adoption and reunion issues. Until recently, it has been all but impossible to even dream of a search or a reunion, let alone to read about it or to talk to others who have blazed the trail.

Given the multitude and the complexity of the issues that arise, it is difficult for a reunitee struggling in isolation to gain a clear perspective of what is happening to her during her post-reunion period. Support systems for both before and after a reunion are integral to a reunion's success. Reunitees need help overcoming the hurdles that precede reunion, and encouragement to share and to explore their post-reunion feelings. A safe environment is needed in which to discuss their new relationships openly and honestly.

For this reason, voluntary search groups that help birth mothers and adoptees find each other have proliferated over the years. Due to a lack of financial and professional resources, however, these groups are seldom equipped to assist the successful reunitee in adjusting to her new relationship over the long term. The overwhelming long-term post-reunion issues have dominated reunitees' initial efforts and many reunions lie dead in the water because they haven't been nurtured. This is particularly unfortunate because with education and adequate supports in place, the post-reunion experience can be a fulfilling one.

The support networks that are available to reunitees include peers, family, search groups (for pre-reunion support), counselling from public agencies, post-adoption reunion support groups, private counsellors and clinics, 12-step support groups and various forms of education. We'll look at each of these more carefully in this chapter.

PEER REUNITEES

Peer counselling is one of the most powerful tools in overcoming the isolation of a reunion. Sometimes, talking to another reunitee will give the adoptee the confidence she needs to go through with her own reunion.

The most helpful step I took before meeting my birth mother was to talk to another adoptee who'd already had a reunion. I'd been to several (mandatory) counselling sessions at the Children's Aid Society, and was scared to death. My reunion was one week away. When I talked to Vince, however, he described his feelings before he met his birth mother, and it felt as though he were reading my mind.

One 40-year-old adoptee wrote to me after I'd encouraged him to continue his search: "Because of your involvement I finally found my mother and know about my father. But most of all, I know about me. I know we only met briefly a couple of times, but you gave me the incentive I needed to push on."

I've met with birth mothers and adoptees on an informal basis, at their request, for several years, and find it a wonderful experience. Hearing about their fears and struggles reassures me that I'm not alone with mine. Being able to share their feelings gives them the support they need. Often, they have no one else to talk to who can understand what they're experiencing.

Adoptive parents of adult children may benefit from attending a support group comprised of people who have recently adopted children. Today's adoptive parents, who have been educated regarding the possibility of a reunion for their adopted child, may be able to cast new light on reunion issues to adoptive parents whose son or daughter is now an adult and is considering, or is having, a reunion. Young adoptive parents, through sharing their own feelings about reunions, will be able to educate yesterday's adoptive parents and to support them as they try to put the reunion into perspective.

FAMILY

While one might think one's family would be the first place to look for support, those closest to adoptees or birth mothers are often the least willing to discuss a reunion, because of their own fears, insecurities or lack of familiarity with reunion issues.

Sometimes a spouse or child is instinctively supportive. However, it usually takes a while for all family members to become educated and comfortable with the issues surrounding the reunion. As a result of a reunion, the reunitee's spouse and children will have to reevaluate their place in the reunitee's life, and often it is they who need reassurance that they are still loved and important to the reunitee after her reunion.

Gord remembers his adoptive parents' silence regarding his upcoming reunion with his birth mother. "They didn't mean to hurt me," says Gord, "but they just didn't understand. I remember the day before my reunion. No one was talking about it at my house. My mom was very threatened. It was like a black cloud floating over the house for a while."

Even when adoptive families wish to be supportive, often adoptees are unwilling to share their feelings with adoptive parents for fear of hurting them. Loyalty issues are prominent in the minds of adoptees, who try to protect their adoptive parents while pursuing their need for a reunion. Sadly, sometimes the adoptee's isolation from the adoptive family is self-imposed and unnecessary. Adoptees, too, have to be encouraged to overcome their fears and to confide in family members, who may prove to be understanding and supportive if given the chance.

Adoptive families' needs must also be considered for the reunion to be successful. In an (unpublished) study, Webber, Thompson and Stoneman observe, "The members of the triad who appear to feel the most vulnerable are the adoptive parents and it is clear that there is a need for some outreach to this group so that they may feel less betrayed." Even fewer resources are available for this group, who, ironically, were once considered the "recipients" of the adoption service and are today left hanging with their fears about their adoptive child's reunion with her birth family.

SEARCH GROUPS

It's usually easier to find a group of people who are hoping for a reunion, rather than a group of people who have already had one. As we've seen, Parent Finders is a volunteer organization that helps adoptees and birth parents to locate one another.

Meeting a birth family member is not the same as meeting a new friend. As adoptee Jackie explains, "If you lose a friend, you lose a friend. But there's a blood tie here. There's a heart tie, an emotional tie. It's family ... my birth family. You can always make new friends, but you won't always make a new family."

Rosemary remembers the support she got from her Parent Finders group after she'd found her birth daughter. She'd planned to attend a meeting with her birth daughter to surprise the other members.

"Only a couple of people at Parent Finders knew that I'd found her and met her. Somebody must have got on the phone and said that there was something special happening that night at the meeting, because there were about 40 people there. I thought, 'This isn't an average meeting. What's going on?'

"When the meeting started, they asked if anyone had any news. I wanted to shout, 'I do!' but I waited as we went around the circle. Then when I was telling my story, I started to cry. There was a birth mother on either side of me and they were both hanging onto my hands. The tears were so thick, we could have swam away. I said, 'I'd like you to meet my daughter whom I finally met.' By then, I'd say 35 out of the 40 people there were bawling their eyes out. They gave Joanne and me each a long-stemmed red rose."

Adoptive parents might wish to consider attending a Parent Finders meeting to educate themselves about reunion issues. Hearing the stories of other adoptees might help them to better understand their own adoptive son's or daughter's desire for a reunion, and to know how to talk to him or her concerning their feelings about the search and reunion.

COUNSELLING FROM PUBLIC AGENCIES

While public agencies that facilitate adoptions and provide non-identifying information vary widely in their practices, some do provide support to their post-adoption clients.

An example is the Children's Aid Society of London and Middlesex, Ontario, which requests that clients come to the agency to receive their non-identifying information. This is because, says social worker Cathy Basile, even a "typical" history, with a young, single mother and father who didn't marry, is very traumatic. Sending this information through the mail (as is sometimes done) can be both devastating and inappropriate.

When the client comes in to receive this information, says Basile, "We try to interpret for the adoptee the birth parents' role and the circumstances in the communities at the time, to prepare them for the reasons why their adoption occurred."

Public adoption agencies also facilitate reunions. Once an adoptee and a birth family member have both registered at a provincial adoption registry, a social worker at a public adoption agency receives notification and begins preliminary work on the case. The parties to the match are then notified by mail. In Manitoba and Ontario, counselling is mandatory by law before identifying information can be released.

Of mandatory counselling, social worker Mary Beth Hoy says, "It's not going to be very effective if the person's there because you're holding a gun to their head."

Pat Richardson, an adoptee and member of the Canadian Adoption Reunion and Registry Search and Support Group (CARR), also takes a stance against mandatory counselling. Speaking on behalf of adoptees, she says, "I think we should be free to have the counselling we want, to phone up and ask for it, but not be forced to have it."

Basile agrees that counselling is lost on some clients. "There are 20 to 30 percent of my clients with whom I feel I haven't had an impact. They're not listening to me. They want to get the counselling over and done with, because they think, 'None of this is going to happen to me.' In that situation, I have to go ahead with the reunion because I have no legal right to say they can't, even though I know they're headed for trouble."

Despite controversy and ethical concerns, counselling has been deemed helpful by social workers and their clients. I feel that the input provided by a social worker before my reunion was important. It was not so much "counselling" that I received, but rather education, support and the background information I needed to proceed with my reunion.

Being legally compelled to visit a Children's Aid Society office to have a reunion has some negative aspects. I felt disempowered by the many factors over which I did not have control in my reunion. My social worker received the letters from my birth mother before I did, and therefore controlled when I would receive them. She read the letters before I did (and, I now know from having worked at a CAS, so do other workers in some cases). Social workers also determine when the reunion takes place, based on their own schedule of holidays and their availability. In my case, my social worker made every effort to be as flexible as possible, which helped me to feel less overpowered by the "system."

Cathy Basile feels that the social worker's role is to put the reunion process in perspective. Initially, says Basile, adoptees think that their birth mother is waiting in the next room, and that the counsellor is just there to make the introductions and then the whole process will be over and done with. In reality, a reunion may take weeks to months, depending on how far apart the clients live, when they feel emotionally prepared to meet, and when the social workers involved can schedule appointments.

Part of Basile's function, she says, is to "gauge the timing of the process, either to speed it up or to slow it down, depending on the client."

Counselling after a reunion is not mandatory, and in British Columbia post-reunion counselling is not available. In other provinces, it varies in availability from agency to agency. Basile incorporates one post-reunion counselling appointment into her practice as a follow-up to the reunion. This allows reunitees to talk about their feelings and to seek advice. Yet in the initial weeks of a reunion, most clients are not ready to discuss their feelings, and many are on a "high" from their reunion and haven't yet run into snags. Only after the initial honeymoon period subsides do reunitees begin to realize the difficulties of their reunion and, in some cases, to seek post-reunion counselling.

Post-reunion counselling services, even where available, are not advertised, due to a lack of both funding and qualified workers. Frequently, clients are either unaware of these services or are unwilling to share their feelings about the reunion with a social worker whom they feel they know only marginally, and sometimes superficially, at best. Even if a reunitee does want help, the lack of training and experience for workers in the field remains a problem. In addition, those who haven't actually experienced a reunion are often ill-equipped to deal with post-reunion issues.

PRIVATE COUNSELLORS

Research on post-reunion issues is sorely lacking, and education for professional counsellors in this area reflects this fact. Some private counsellors, however, may have sufficient expertise to enable them to handle the very specific needs of adoption clients. Particularly helpful are grief counsellors and any therapists who can help reunion clients to express the unresolved past emotions triggered by their reunions.

For adoptees, these past emotions may have been initiated in the pre-verbal stage of life. Adoptees typically suffer at least three painful separations in infancy: the separation from both their birth families, and at least one separation from their subsequent primary caregiver, usually a foster family. These early crises leave emotional wounds that are often torn open during the post-reunion period. Because post-reunion difficulties began in infancy and are of a very primal nature — such as issues of rejection, abandonment and identity formation — adoptees need an especially safe environment that will allow them to be vulnerable enough to express the feelings associated with their adoption and reunion.

Talking about these feelings may not always be the easiest way to soothe the pain. Indeed, if the problem began in the pre-verbal stage, talking about it may not even be possible. Various forms of therapy — such as art therapy, rebirthing, hypnosis, dream work, Reiki, body work, and writing with the non-dominant hand — can all be effective in tapping into deeply buried feelings, and help the client to reexperience them and release them. These techniques will be beneficial only if the practitioner is experienced and is fully trusted by the adoptee, and provides a safe, private and nurturing environment for the counselling sessions.

When selecting a therapist, it's important to get a referral from a past client who can attest to the therapist's competence. It might also be valuable to get a referral from a physician, if possible. It's also important, especially when exploring non-conventional therapies such as those mentioned above, to educate oneself about the therapy and its theoretical principles and goals.

Clinics equipped specifically to handle adoption and reunion issues exist in the United States. One such clinic is The Family Center, in Somerville, Massachusetts. The Center is run by Dr. Joyce Maguire Pavao. Dr. Pavao works with a team of professionals on issues affecting the life cycle of the adoptive family, including pre- and post-reunion problems. Pavao has been working in the field of adoption for nearly 20 years and was herself adopted at ten days old.

Since Pavao's clinic is private, fees are charged for services. The price is a small one to pay, however, for access to Pavao and her colleagues' rich experience and insights regarding adoption issues.

Similar clinics that deal with adoption and post-adoption, including reunions, exist throughout the United States, including Adoption Crossroads Counselling Center in New York City, Adoption Support and Enrichment Services in Franklin and Farmingham, Massachusetts, and Parenting Resources in Tustin, California. At the time of this book's publication, comparable clinics do not yet exist in Canada.

POST-ADOPTION REUNION SUPPORT GROUP (PAR) AS PROTOTYPE

The Post-Adoption Reunion Support Group (PAR) consists of about eight to ten adoptees and birth parents who have had reunions. They meet weekly to offer support to each other, to discuss their feelings about their reunions, and to explore post-reunion issues. Occasionally, adoptive parents whose adult children have had reunions attend the group to learn more about reunions and to share their own feelings. Although not primarily comprised of adoptive parents, PAR can be a good source of education for them.

Cathy Basile founded and facilitates the group. "The initial premise for founding PAR," says Basile, "was to give people who have had reunions the opportunity to validate their experiences. This group helps the members to confirm for one another that what they're experiencing is not something bizarre or specific to them."

About two years after the establishment of PAR I in 1988, a second group, PAR II was formed; this allowed the original group to continue to explore long-term post-reunion issues. The second group was comprised of newer reunitees who were still experiencing short-term post-reunion difficulties.

"The new people who come into the group are not ready to go into PAR I, the originally established group," says Basile. "In PAR I, they're more ready to talk about the negatives of their experience, whereas in PAR II, everything's still great, but they're starting to see cracks. In PAR II, they're starting to talk about these cracks, but it's really basic stuff like, 'Should I invite them for dinner or shouldn't I?'"

In PAR I, issues such as disliking your counterpart are discussed. Says Basile, "It takes a long time to get to the point where you can say something like that. You're prepared to talk about really serious issues like rejection and sexuality in PAR I, but not in PAR II. Maybe a couple of months down the road, when they get more comfortable with their group, they might be ready for the next phase."

Although agencies across Canada are becoming aware of PAR's existence and interest is generating the formation of new groups, funding and staffing are minimal. PAR, however, has managed to serve as a prototype for other public adoption agencies that are trying to form their own reunitee support groups. When contacted by other professionals in the field, Cathy Basile shares information on an informal basis by telephone regarding her role as facilitator and organizer of the group.

Basile's London, Ontario, PAR groups could well serve as a valuable national resource, were funding available to collate information about the origin, history, mandate, organization and facilitation of the London groups. Unfortunately, this information may be a long time coming as public adoption agencies across the country struggle to keep afloat in tough economic times, and staffing and resources for even basic services dwindle.

There are several features of PAR meetings that distinguish them from other support organizations handling post-adoption reunion issues, such as a 12-step support group. First, a social worker facilitates the meetings. Members have a say in the agenda, and occasionally films or television documentaries discussing different aspects of reunions are shown. Art therapy is sometimes used to unearth buried emotions that would otherwise be difficult to access.

Another unique trait is that PAR's focus is on the emotional aftermath of the reunion. This is not the case in search groups, which are geared towards search mechanics.

The group also supports adoptees who have located, but not yet met, their birth mothers. The PAR group acts as a healthy outlet for the frustrations, grief and fears associated with being put on "hold" by a found birth mother. In addition, various courses of action for these members are discussed, and advice — either encouragement or caution — is provided.

TWELVE-STEP SUPPORT GROUPS

While I am unaware of any similar support groups in Canada, there is a unique group called "Healing Adoption" based in

Bourne, Massachusetts. It's a support group based on the 12-step program used by Alcoholics Anonymous, Overeaters Anonymous and other 12-step groups. This group has intelligently and successfully applied the 12-step philosophy to adoption issues, and their program is worth an overview. Hopefully, similar groups will be formed in Canada. (For contact addresses, please see Appendix D.)

"Healing Adoption" focuses on adoption and reunion "myths and lies," and tries to dispel these, while working towards healing and wholeness for its membership. Here is a partial list of "myths and lies," excerpted from the group's literature:

- We're bad and ungrateful people if we search for our birth family.
- We don't love our adoptive parents if we search for our birth family.
- Knowing our birth family will weaken our adoptive family relationship.
- Talking about our true feelings about adoption will cause us trouble.
- Asking too many questions is a sign of weakness and disre − spect to our adoptive parents.
- Birth mothers don't want their babies.
- Birth parents are bad people.
- Adoption doesn't hurt.
- Adopting a baby cures infertility pain.

Many, if not all, of these statements struck a chord in me when I read them. Many of them stung and all of them were familiar, although I had never seen them laid out so honestly and blatantly before.

The group has compiled a list of topics relevant to adoption, including trust, self-esteem, anger, guilt, intimacy, depression, suicide, and so on. While these issues could be part of any 12-step group discussions, the following discussion topics seem to be tailored specifically to adoption itself: bonding, unwanted pregnancies, fantasies, people-watching, search (including obsession and post-search depression) and how we feel (or do not feel) about our births. These are but a few of the unique topics the group has addressed that seem particularly geared to the needs of adoptees, birth families and adoptive families.

RESEARCH AND EDUCATION

A little education goes a long way. A lot can go even farther in preparing the reunitee for the reunion and its aftermath. As mentioned earlier, networking with other reunitees is often the best education before and after a reunion, but other resources are available as well.

The media, while tending to sensationalize reunions, do sometimes offer valuable information. Television talk shows are notorious for focussing on the fantastic. Unless you want to panic, they should be viewed with some reservations. Better are made-for television movies that sometimes portray the feelings of the reunion more reasonably. An excellent example is the National Film Board of Canada's *Foster Child*, which documents a real-life reunion.

Radio talk shows about reunions can provide a great cross-section of voices, from participants to professionals. CBC Radio has twice aired a two-part series on reunions featuring stories from reunitees.

Conferences and newsletters are also invaluable. Conferences are held across North America; they feature leading professionals in the field of adoption and reunion. There are numerous newsletters available, including the American Adoption Congress's "Decree," and the newsletter of The Adoption Council of Ontario, "Adoption Roundup." Some Parent Finders chapters also produce their own newsletters. To find out more about newsletters, contact any of the groups mentioned in Appendices C and D.

Finally, books about various aspects of adoption are available to help reunitees assimilate their experiences. (See Print Resources at the end of this book.)

It is imperative that universities and colleges in North America update their academic research and curricula to include current adoption and post-adoption theory in relevant disciplines, particularly in social work, psychiatry, medicine and psychology.

In his 1985 report, referred to previously, Ralph Garber says that while social workers involved in the area of abuse receive specialized training, those counselling adoption and post-adoption clients do not receive specialized training — but they should.[27] It is now more than *eight years* since Garber's recommendations, and nothing has been done to update academic curricula.

New curricula should include education about specific adoption-related issues beginning from birth and progressing throughout the life cycle of the adoptee and her birth and adoptive families. Current research in various topics such as genetic inheritance, prenatal and postnatal psychology and child-parent bonding should be incorporated in adoption education.

Highlighting the fact that many birth mothers in the past were denied the right to see their infant after birth and emphasizing the importance of mother-child bonding should comprise part of the education required for professionals who deal with those affected by adoption. According to David Chamberlain, author of *Babies Remember Birth*, the delivery itself has an impact on the child's subsequent psychological health. Chamberlain's and others' work should be used in the education of medical doctors, particularly obstetricians. Prenatal practices should be taught with a view to facilitating happy birth experiences for *all* mothers, including women whose children will be adopted. Emphasis should be placed on the adoptee's and the birth mother's psychological health before, during and after the birth.

The idea that developing infants respond to and benefit from communication before and immediately after birth is gaining popularity in Europe and, more slowly, throughout North America. In response to new theories and data, the International Society of Study of Prenatal Psychology (ISPP) was established in Vienna in 1971. The group, comprised of European psychologists and physicians, is specifically devoted to the study of prenatal psychology.[28]

The combination of support services, education in the field of adoption and progressive adoption practices will help to ensure that both yesterday's and future adoptees and their families will benefit from, and not be hurt by, the practice of adoption.

§

CHAPTER 12

RECOMMENDATIONS FOR CHANGE AND HEALING

As the result of my wish to meet my birth family, I've had to juggle my adoptive family, my birth family and my partner's family at Christmas. I have to remember more birthdays, write more letters and navigate more relationships. Sometimes I wonder if one person can possibly cope with having so many families! While I have no regrets about pursuing my reunion, there are also many aspects I wish I had known about before I began ... not that the knowledge would have deterred me.

My birth mother and I have an on-going relationship, and the times we see each other are warm, genuine and loving. We have had the good fortune to receive on-going support from family and friends. But now I realize that the reunion, rather than an ending, was a beginning, and, like my birth, has changed both our lives forever.

—M. M.

ONE THING I'VE LEARNED from both my own and others' reunions is that the future is unpredictable and the bottom line in reunions is to never give up.

As I write these words, I can happily report that Jackie, the 32-year-old adoptee we first met in Chapter 6, has now met her birth mother. Jackie first learned her birth mother's address in 1985. In 1992, seven years, several phone calls, various letters and a million tears later, Jackie finally had a face-to-face meeting with her birth mother.

Jackie's story is not unusual. Because reunions are a relatively new phenomenon and dramatically overturn the foundation upon which yesterday's closed adoptions were built, it can take birth mothers or other family members several years to deal with unresolved issues and new dilemmas that a potential reunion with the adoptee represents.

Patience, kindness and understanding are the key to weathering the trials of a lengthy search and reunion. But more than once, I've seen what looked like a hopeless situation, as in Jackie's case, suddenly turn around and become a happy and mutually rewarding reunion. Had Jackie not had the wisdom and patience to wait until her birth mother was ready, this may not have happened.

Even after a happy meeting, as we've seen, difficulties develop. Six years after my own reunion, there is still so much missing for me that I continue to want to retrieve the whole story. Having lost the beginning of their stories, adoptees can become obsessed with the past and with their need to know details of their family's history and of their own birth. Many, like myself, feel unable to go on with their lives until they've reviewed every detail and nuance of their past, many times. As adoptees, we haven't had the experience of growing up with the knowledge of our origins. Thus, as adults, it takes time for this new information to become an intrinsic part of our identity. Not knowing your past imprisons you in psychological and emotional stasis. How can you go forward if you don't know where you come from?

Recently, I watched my birth mother waltzing with her

mother, my birth grandmother, in my birth grandmother's living room. They danced beautifully together and I found myself envying the continuity of their relationship, their history, which reached back generations, long before either of their births. The sight amazed me, and as I watched, my eyes watered and I realized how much I had missed and how much I still didn't know. Then my grandmother reached for my hand and I awkwardly stumbled around her rug, unable to match the elegance of her and her daughter. Here I was, dancing with the grandmother I never knew — and perhaps would never really know.

I don't think my grandmother has any idea how important she is to me. I have heard a few stories of her home, her life and her loves, and look forward to learning more. It struck me then that my adoption, and, more importantly, my feelings about it, are still taboo subjects. I have no idea how my birth grandmother and birth grandfather, my only living grandparents, feel about having their daughter's relinquished child in their living room, sipping tea and eating birthday cake to celebrate my birth grandfather's 87th birthday. I'd love to know their feelings and I hope to have the courage to be more open with them some day.

I feel a strong need to break my silence, to speak the truth, and to share on a deeper level so that we might have an honest relationship. Even though we are reunited, I do not want to indulge in the fantasy that I have always been a member of my birth family, ignoring the pain that came with my adoption and, now, with my reunion. This kind of pretending only causes further pain for me, and I've already paid the price of a closed adoption. Reunions are only one step towards healing the pain.

LEGISLATIVE CHANGES

To improve adoption practice, one change that should be made immediately is the implementation of legislation that supports the current trend towards open adoptions. Today's fledgling efforts towards open adoption are not buttressed by legislation and, therefore, leave professionals and participants confused and stymied in their efforts to update adoption practice. Changes in adoption legislation should be made consistent in every province, in order to standardize adoption practice and to give adoptees, birth families and adoptive families equal rights across the country.

Birth parents in all provinces today continue to lose all legal rights to their children once the adoption has been legally finalized by the courts. Even in cases where the adoptive family agrees to communicate regularly with the birth family, the adoptive family understandably wishes to go on with their lives as a "normal" family after the adoption has been finalized. This attitude, however, can come dangerously close to maintaining the denial that characterized adoption in the past. It is integral to the health of adoptive family members to keep in mind, as adoptees grows older, that the adoptee has a genetic and social heritage that is different from and as rich as their own. Adoption participants, past and present, must come to recognize that birth families cannot be replaced by adoptive families, and vice versa. They are, by definition, not interchangeable and each has unique gifts to offer the adoptee.

Legislation is needed to make agreements of ongoing contact legally binding for all parties. This is not unlike the courts' responsibility to ensure child support payments from separated and divorced partners; the child's best interests must be upheld. Just as it is now recognized that adoption is a lifelong process, it follows that counselling should be available to all adoption participants — birth parents, adoptive parents and adoptees — on an on-going basis, providing both information and support.

For the sake of the adoptee's psychological health, it is valid to compel adoptive parents through legislation, to tell their children that they were adopted. Adoptees remain vulnerable to adoptive parents who would rather substitute the stork, the cabbage patch, the adoption agency or the adoptive mother for the birth mother. While it would be impossible to enforce such a law, it would nevertheless serve to reinforce a healthier and more realistic perspective on adoption practice, one that advocates psychological health rather than the irrationality and fears of the past.

Today's adoption legislation and practice should recognize that bearing a child entails at least a minimal amount of responsibility to that child, even if the birth mother wants nothing further to do with her child after the birth. At the very least, information about the adoptee's ethnic origin; a physical description and a mental and physical profile of the birth family; number of siblings or half-siblings related to the adoptee; place, time and details of her birth; the adoptee's family tree; the religion, interests, aptitudes and educational levels of the ancestral family — all are the adoptee's birthright and all are necessary for a healthy personal identity. Growing up without this information, as we've seen, puts the adoptee at a tremendous disadvantage.

There is still no legislation ensuring that information provided by birth families is accurate. In recognizing parenthood as involving responsibility, and background information as a basic human right, legislation should stipulate that birth parents are legally responsible to provide verifiable background information for the adoptee before the child is adopted. In addition to medical and other descriptive information, the reasons for the adoption should be outlined, clearly and honestly.

Currently, when background information is provided to

adult adoptees, at their request, it is dispensed at the discretion of social workers. This practice is patronizing and condescending. Although adoptees are adults and are legally entitled to their background information, they remain disempowered by the judgments of others. In many, if not most, cases, those sharing the information with the adoptee have a superficial relationship with them at best, yet these people are in a position of power in which they can decide what an adoptee can or cannot "handle."

On occasion, unpleasant details in the adoptee's past are diluted by euphemisms or are omitted entirely. This practice further perpetuates the infantilization and disempowerment of adoptees, who have no other source from which to request this information and who remain at the mercy of the social worker's subjective judgment. This practice begs the question: From whom is the adoptee being protected? Pavao[29] and other researchers concur that adult adoptees have a right to receive all the available facts about their adoption and birth families, not just those a social worker deems relevant or palatable.

Some adoptees conduct their own searches, using their background information as clues. It's particularly dangerous for an adoptee whose background information omitted volatile, negative or crime-related information to pursue a reunion, without being properly prepared. In this case, the adoptee may be in for an unpleasant, or, at worst, dangerous meeting. Ironically, the information may have been withheld in the adoptee's "best interests."

RETAINING LEGAL USE OF ONE'S BIRTH NAME

Another step towards helping an adoptee resolve her identity conflicts, in addition to providing accurate background information, is to give her the legal right to use both or either of her names — birth and adoptive. Few of today's adult adoptees know their original names. Some don't even realize they had a name before their adoption. The reality is that adoptees are not born with their adoptive names. This may seem like a niggling semantic point, but the practice of legally issuing new birth certificates to adoptees is the ultimate symbol of the whole erase-the-past approach of closed adoptions.

Choosing to retain, incorporate or revert to a birth name is a way for adoptees to integrate their past with their present. It is symbolic of wholeness, of a way to bring together the various aspects of their identity, acknowledging both genetic and environmental influences while honouring both sets of parents. Adoptees, who had no say in the original decision to be adopted, can reclaim some measure of control over their lives by choosing which name or names they will use. Many more women have begun to retain their maiden names after marriage, or to hyphenate their surname with their spouse's. This practice is based on the same principle of retaining your own personhood, your own identity.

CAREFUL PLACEMENT

As we see proof of the genetic component in personality, intelligence, aptitude, and so on, these factors must be taken into consideration when placing infants in adoptive homes. An adoptee who is placed in an adoptive home whose family members share the temperaments, interests, value systems, philosophy and aptitudes of the birth family, and who has an open or semi-open adoption, may be less likely to suffer the "alien" feeling so familiar to adoptees who were placed under the past regime.

Open adoption which retains a continual link with the birth families, both maternal and paternal, is the best way to enable an adoptee to develop a solid identity. In adoptions that remain closed or semi-closed, careful interviews of the extended birth family before the adoption become even more important, in order to provide the adoptive family with a comprehensive picture of the adoptee's family of origin. The child could then be placed in an adoptive family that is fully informed and accepting of the birth family, and that may resemble the birth family in terms of interests, aptitudes, personalities, and so on.

It is important that when birth families and adoptive families diverge, the adoptive family shares that information completely with the adoptee. For example, an adoptee whose ethnic and/or racial origins differ from the adoptive family's should be fully educated about the customs, religion and culture of her birth family. This would contribute to the adoptee's healthy identity formation as well as better prepare her for an eventual reunion, should she seek or be sought by a birth family member.

NATIONAL ADOPTION DISCLOSURE REGISTRY

In trying to grapple with legislative inconsistency, there have been many calls for change in Canadian laws governing adoption and post-adoption. Paul Sachdev, a professor at Memorial University in Newfoundland, is a researcher in post-reunions and the author of *Adoption: Current Issues and Trends*. In a 1988 editorial in *The Globe and Mail*, a Toronto-based daily newspaper, Sachdev recommends a national registry to which birth mothers and adoptees could apply.

A national adoption disclosure registry would circumvent the tedium and expense of social agencies that must communicate across the country for even the most rudimentary information. Such a registry would serve as a central information bank, replacing the haphazard system that exists today, where information, both identifying and non-identifying, is scattered among social service agencies, provincial registries, and private adoption workers and clinics.

The one national registry that exists, run by Parent Finders, serves only Parent Finders members and does not provide background information or pre-or post-reunion counselling.

The problem of differing legislation in each province could be partially alleviated if there were a central national adoption disclosure registry. A centralized registry would provide searches for all birth family members and adoptees. This would be an important improvement on the current situation, in which birth mothers and adoptees in some provinces can search through provincial registries but others cannot, because services do not exist in their province. Centralization would also ensure that the service is provided for free or for an equal set fee for everyone.

A central registry would not solve the problem of the lack of counselling and support services in each province. These services could be facilitated by support groups comprised of reunitees themselves and professionals who are educated in the field of adoption.

A CHANGING SOCIETY

Underlying these proposed changes in adoption practice and legislation is the need for profound social change. North American culture is currently undergoing dramatic changes in every realm, changes that affect our religious, social, educational, family and workplace institutions. As we begin to identify how these institutions are no longer meeting our needs and the ways in which they have been destructive, we must strive for truth and honesty in order to achieve healthier relationships with ourselves, our families, our communities, and our shared mother, the Earth.

In place of fear and shame, deception and illusions, repression and anger, we must put love, trust, mutual respect and co-operation. Only in this type of environment can the practice of adoption flourish as a healthy parenting alternative.

Adoptive parents must be provided with the facts, not fallacies, of human development. The need for knowledge of one's genetic heritage must be recognized. Adoptive parents must be encouraged and helped to work through the unique issues confronting them.

Women and men must work together to eliminate the stigma of the "unwed mother." Men must be supported in their rights and their role as birth father and encouraged to participate fully in planning for their children, while acknowledging a woman's ultimate right to her own body and its functions, including the birth process. Men must be held responsible for their role in procreation and they must be allowed to explore their feelings surrounding the issues of an unplanned pregnancy. It is only through self-knowledge and self-examination that we can, as individuals and as a culture, move forward, towards a more sane and supportive society.

More emphasis must be placed on the availability of birth control methods and the dissemination of information about birth control practices. Adoption, at its best, provides only a second-rate solution. To some degree, adoptees *by definition* will continue to feel rejected, will still wonder why they weren't raised by their birth families, will still wince when asked in a routine checkup for their medical history — if they don't have the answers. They'll continue to fear, for good reason, for their own children's safety if they have no knowledge of their medical background. Birth mothers will miss the experience of raising their child, even while ostensibly benefiting from freedom from motherhood, whether or not they desired that freedom or had it forced upon them by circumstances beyond their control.

As adoptees and birth families meet, healing can take place. Today's proliferation of support groups bears witness to the fact that this is a transformative age. The damage we've foisted on each other has manifested itself in our society's careless destruction of our planet; in violence and callousness; and in neglect and physical, psychological and sexual abuse of our children. As these phenomena escalate, there is nevertheless a desperate struggle for survival as we strive to find solutions before it's too late.

A culture such as ours, which has a multitude of self-help and support groups — adult children of alcoholics, incest survivors' groups, gay rights groups, and a plethora of 12-step programs — already has fertile soil upon which the acceptance of post-adoption reunions can grow. The goal of each of these groups is to heal and empower its participants, a goal that is shared by many reunitees.

Alongside many other self-help groups providing support and opportunities for personal growth, post-adoption support groups help reunitees to complete their emotional and psychological development and to claim their birthright as fully integrated human beings, with a present, a future *and* a past.

May we succeed in healing ourselves, each other and our planet.

§

APPENDIX A

CANADIAN ADOPTION DISCLOSURE REGISTRIES

	Adoptee's Age to Register	Fee	Search For 65 + First	Pre-Reunion Counselling	Post-Reunion Counselling	Year Registry Began	Searches Available	Year Searches Began
NFLD.	19	NO	NO	OPTIONAL	YES	1983	YES	1990
N. SCOTIA	19	NO	NO	OPTIONAL	YES	1981	YES	1981
N. BRUNS.	19	NO	NO	OPTIONAL	YES	1981	YES	1989
ONTARIO	18	NO	NO	MANDATORY	YES	1979	YES	1987
MANITOBA	18	NO	YES	MANDATORY	YES	1981	YES	1986
SASK.	18	YES	YES	OPTIONAL	YES	1970	YES	1982
ALBERTA	18	NO	N/A	OPTIONAL	YES	1985	NO	N/A
B.C.*	19	YES	NO	NOT AVB	NO	1987	YES	1991
YUKON	19	NO	N/A	OPTIONAL	YES	1984	NO	N/A
P.E.I.**								
QUEBEC**	N/A	NO	N/A	OPTIONAL	YES	N/A	N/A	N/A
N.W.T.**	18	NO	N/A	OPTIONAL	YES	N/A	YES	1985

*Searches available for birth parents and adoptees   ** NO CENTRAL REGISTRY — contact agency where adoption was completed for services

CANADIAN ADOPTION DISCLOSURE REGISTRIES

NEWFOUNDLAND

Department of Social Services, 3rd
Flr., Confederation Bldg.
P.O. Box 4750
ST. JOHN'S, Newfoundland
A1C 5T7 (709) 576-2667

NOVA SCOTIA

Director, Family and Children's
Services
Department of Community Services
P.O. Box 696
HALIFAX, Nova Scotia B3J 2T7
(902) 424-3202

NEW BRUNSWICK

Post Adoption Services
Department of Health and
Community Services
P.O. Box 5100
FREDERICTON, New Brunswick
E3B 5G8
(506) 453-2949

ONTARIO

The Adoption Unit
2 Bloor Street W., 24th Flr.
TORONTO, Ontario M7A 1E9
(416) 327-4690

MANITOBA

Post-Adoption Registry
2nd Flr., 114 Garry Street
WINNIPEG, Manitoba R3C 1G1
(204) 945-6962
Toll Free 1-800-282-8060

SASKATCHEWAN

Provincial Adoption Registry
207-2240 Albert Street
REGINA, Saskatchewan S4P 3V7
(306) 787-3654
Toll Free 1-800-667-7539

ALBERTA

Post-Adoption Registry
9th Flr., 7th Street Plaza
10030 — 107 Street
EDMONTON, Alberta T5J 3E4
(403) 427-6387

BRITISH COLUMBIA

Ministry of Health
Adoption Reunion Registry
Division of Vital Statistics
1515 Blanshard Street
VICTORIA, British Columbia
V8W 3C8 (604) 387-0041

YUKON

Family and Children's Services
Placement and Support Services
Supervisor
Department of Health and Human
Resources
P.O. Box 2703
WHITEHORSE, Yukon Y1A 2C6
(403) 667-3002

P.E.I.

Coordinator, Children in Care
Health and Social Services
P.O. Box 2000
CHARLOTTETOWN, Prince Edward
Island C1A 7N5 (902) 368-4931

QUEBEC

Ville Marie Social Service Centre
5 Weredale Park
MONTREAL, Quebec H3Z 1Y5
(514) 935-6196

OR CONTACT INDIVIDUAL
PUBLIC AGENCY

N.W.T.

Program Officer
Family and Children's Services
Department of Social Services
Box 1320
Government of Northwest
Territories
YELLOWKNIFE, Northwest
Territories X1A 2L9
(403) 873-7943

PARENT FINDERS NATIONAL
REGISTRY

c/o Ms. Joan E. Vanstone
3960 Westridge Avenue
WEST VANCOUVER, British
Columbia V7V 3H7
(604) 926-1096

PARENT FINDERS CONTACTS

CANADA:

NOVA SCOTIA
Parent Finders
Box 4, Site 35, R.R. 2
TANTALLON, Nova Scotia B0J 3J0

NEW BRUNSWICK
Parent Finders
P.O. Box 263
ROTHESAY, New Brunswick
E0G 2W0
(506) 847-8098

ONTARIO
Parent Finders
36 Woodbridge Road
HAMILTON, Ontario L8K 3C9
(416) 522-8644

Parent Finders Inc.
Ste. 11, 2279 Yonge Street
TORONTO, Ontario M4P 2C7
(416) 760-7759

Parent Finders
Apt. 112, 305 Briarhill Street
LONDON, Ontario N5Y 4V8
(519) 434-7120

Parent Finders
146 Richmond Street
THOROLD, Ontario L2V 3H4
(416) 227-6251

Parent Finders
P.O. Box 35
COTTAM, Ontario N0R 1B0

Parent Finders — National Capital
Region
P.O. Box 5211, Postal Station "F"
OTTAWA, Ontario K2C 3H5
(613) 825-6256

SASKATCHEWAN
Parent Finders
P.O. Box 123
MERVIN, Saskatchewan S0M 1Y0

ALBERTA
Parent Finders
P.O. Box 12031
EDMONTON, Alberta T5J 3L2
(403) 466-3335

Parent Finders
18 Oslo Close
RED DEER, Alberta T4N 5A5

BRITISH COLUMBIA
Parent Finders
3960 Westridge Avenue
WEST VANCOUVER, British
Columbia V7V 3H7
(604) 524-8011

Parent Finders
P.O. Box 1991
HOPE, British Columbia V0X 1L0
(604) 869-7254

Parent Finders
Box 84, Main Postal Station
KAMLOOPS, British Columbia
V2C 5K3

Parent Finders
1062 Maple Close
QUESNEL, British Columbia
V2J 3W3
(604) 747-2323

Parent Finders
4152 Chestnut Drive
PRINCE GEORGE, British Columbia
V2K 2T5

Parent Finders
Box 7051, Depot #4
VICTORIA, British Columbia
V9B 4Z2
(604) 642-6122

P.E.I.

Parent Finders
R.R. #2
NORTH WILTSHIRE, Prince Edward
Island C0A 1Y0
(705) 522-8178

U.S.A.:

MICHIGAN

Parent Finders
1602 Cole
BIRMINGHAM, Michigan 48008

Parent Finders
P.O. Box 52, Old Westbury
LONG ISLAND, New York 11568

AFFILIATED ADOPTION GROUPS

CANADA:

ONTARIO

Canadian Adoption Reunion
Register Search and Support
Group (CARR)
63 Welland Avenue
TORONTO, Ontario M4T 2H9

ALBERTA

Birthparents/Relatives Group
3908-118 Avenue
EDMONTON, Alberta T5W 5E1
(403) 478-0197

BRITISH COLUMBIA

Forget Me Not Family Society
Box 61526, Brookswood Post
Office
LANGLEY, British Columbia
V3A 8C8
(604) 530-2160

TRIAD

432 Obed Avenue
VICTORIA, British Columbia
V9A 1K5
(604) 385-7884

Cariboo Adoption Support Group
25-803 Hodgson Road
WILLIAMS LAKE, British Columbia
V2G 3R2
(604) 392-4282

Adoptees & Birthparents
600 Jaschinsky Road
KELOWNA, British Columbia
V1X 1L8 (604) 860-5368

U.S.A.:

CALIFORNIA

Triadoption Library
Box 638
WESTMINSTER, California 92683

Parenting Resources
250 El Camino Real, Suite 111
TUSTIN, California 82680
(714) 669-8100

COLORADO

Orphan Voyage
2141 Road 2300
CEDAREDGE, Colorado 81413
(303) 856-3937

MASSACHUSETTS

The Family Center Inc.
Pre and Post Adoption Consulting
Team (PACT)
385 Highland Avenue
W.SOMERVILLE, Massachusetts
02144
(617) 628-8815

Healing Adoption
BOURNE, Massachusetts
(508) 224-3953, (508) 833-1516 or
(508) 295-2346

NEVADA

International Soundex Reunion
Registry
P.O. Box 2312
CARSON CITY, Nevada 89701
(702) 882-6270

NEW JERSEY

Adoptive Parents for Open Records
P.O. Box 193
LONG VALLEY, New Jersey 07853
(908) 850-1706

NEW YORK

American Adoption Congress
P.O. Box 20137, Cherokee Station
NEW YORK, New York 10028

Council For Equal Rights in
Adoption (C.E.R.A.)
401 East 74th Street, Suite 17D
NEW YORK, New York 10021-3919
(212) 988-0110

Adoption Crossroads Counselling
Centre
401 E. 74th Street
NEW YORK, New York 10021-3919
(212) 988-0110

U.K.:

LONDON

Ariel Bruce Associates (Private
Searchers)
6 Regent Square
LONDON, England WC1 H8HZ
071-833-2969

PLEASE CONTACT C.E.R.A. FOR ADDITIONAL CONTACTS

FOOTNOTES

INTRODUCTION

1. Archives of General Psychiatry, 3: 31-32, Marshal D.Schecter, Observation on adopted children, in "A Study of the Themes that Appear in a Clinical Population of Adolescent Adoptees," Joyce Maguire Pavao, Thesis Presented to the Faculty of the Graduate School of Education of Harvard University, 1989, p. 19.

CHAPTER 1

2. Disclosure of Adoption Information, Report of the Special Commissioner, Ralph Garber, D.S.W., Ontario Ministry of Community and Social Services, ("The Garber Report"), Nov. 1985, p. 1.

3. *Unlocking the Adoption Files*, Paul Sachdev, Ph.D., The Free Press, New York, New York, U.S.A., 1990, p. 149.

4. "A Study of the Themes that Appear in a Clinical Population of Adolescent Adoptees," Joyce Maguire Pavao, Thesis Presented to the Faculty of the Graduate School of Education of Harvard University, 1989, p. 15.

5. "Adoption Reunion: A Struggle in Uncharted Relationships," Joan Webber, Jan Thompson, Lou Stoneman, p. 2.

6. *The Globe and Mail*, "Newborns go with dollar flow," Nov. 30, 1992.

7. *After the Adoption*, Elizabeth Hormann, Fleming H. Revell

Company, Old Tappan, New Jersey, U.S.A., 1987, p. 166.

8. *Babies Remember Birth*, David B. Chamberlain, Ph.D.,Jeremy P. Tarcher, Inc., Los Angeles, California, U.S.A., 1988, p. 29.

9. Ibid, pp. 48-49.

10. *The Globe and Mail*, "Newborns go with dollar flow," Nov. 30, 1992.

11. Ibid.

CHAPTER 2

12. Dr. P.A. Vernon, Director of Western Ontario Adoption Project, The University of Western Ontario, London, Ontario, 1987; ongoing study of adoptees and their birth families.

13. Also see *Family Process*, "Birth Parents Who Relinquished Babies for Adoption Revisited," Reuben Pannor, M.S.W., Annette Baran, M.S.W., Arthur Sorosky, M.D., Vol. 17, Sept. 1978, p. 335.

14. *The Other Mother*, Carol Schaefer, Soho Press Inc., New York, New York, U.S.A., 1991, pp. 23-24.

15. Ibid, p. 24.

16. The Garber Report, p. 12.

17. Ibid, p. 12.

CHAPTER 3

18. The Garber Report, p. 13.

19. Thomas J. Bouchard, Minnesota Center for Twin and Adoption Research, Minneapolis, Minnesota, U.S.A.

CHAPTER 5

20. "Adoption Reunion: A Struggle in Uncharted Relationships," Joan Webber, Jan Thompson, Lou Stoneman, p. 8.

CHAPTER 6

21. "Points to Consider in Your Plan to Begin Searching," unpublished document, Mary Beth Hoy, London, Ontario.

22. *Public Welfare*, Lee H. Campbell, "The Birthparent's Right to Know," Summer, 1979, p. 23.

CHAPTER 8

23. "Genetic Sexual Attraction," unpublished article, Barbara Gonyo.

CHAPTER 9

24. *Family Process*, Reuben Pannor, Annette Baran and Arthur D. Sorosky, "Birth Parents Who Relinquished Babies For Adoption Revisited," Vol. 17(3), Sept. 1978, p. 334.

CHAPTER 10

25. *Birthbond*, Judith S. Gediman and Linda P. Brown, New Horizon Press, Far Hills, New Jersey, U.S.A., 1989, p. 139.

26. Dr. P.A. Vernon, Director of Western Ontario Adoption Project, The University of Western Ontario, London, Ontario, 1987; ongoing study of adoptees and their birth families.

CHAPTER 11

27. The Garber Report, p. 49.

28. *Babies Remember Birth*, p. xxiv.

CHAPTER 12

29. Joyce Pavao, speaking at "Adoptions and Reunions: Lifetime Issues of the Adoption Process," Conference, London, Ontario, March, 1991.

REFERENCES

Allen, Madelene. 1992. *Reunion — The Search for My Birth Family*. Toronto: Stoddart Publishing Co.

Andersen, Robert S. M.D . 1988. "Why Adoptees Search: Motives and More." *Child Welfare* Vol.LXVII/1(January/February), 15-19.

Andrews, Roberta G. 1979. "A Clinical Appraisal of Searching," *Public Welfare* Vol. 37/3 (Summer), 15-21.

Arms, Suzanne. 1983. *To Love and Let Go*. New York: Alfred E. Knopf.

Baran, A., Pannor, R. and A.D. Sorosky. 1978. "Birth Parents Who Relinquished Babies for Adoption Revisited." *Family Process* Vol. 17/3 (September), 329-337.

_____. 1975. "Secret Adoption Records: The Dilemma of Our Adoptees." *Psychology Today* (December), 38-42, 96-98.

Biracree, Tom and Nancy. 1989. *The Parents' Book of Facts, Child Development from birth to age five*. New York: Facts on File Inc.

Bouchard, Thomas J. Minnesota Center for Twin and Adoption Research, Minneapolis, Minnesota, ongoing study.

Campbell Lee H. 1979. "The Birthparent's Right to Know." *Public Welfare* Vol. 37/3 (Summer), 22-27.

Chamberlain, David B., Ph.D. 1988. *Babies Remember Birth*. Los Angeles: Jeremy P. Tarcher, Inc.

Clark, Barry. 1989. *My Search For Catherine Anne.* Toronto: James Lorimer & Co. Publishers.

Depp, Carole Hope M.S.W. 1982. "After Reunion: Perceptions of Adult Adoptees, Adoptive Parents, and Birth Parents," *Child Welfare* Vol. 61/ 2, 115-119.

Ensminger, Raymond O. 1984."Adoption Reunions — An Emotional Triangle:Some Background." *The Social Worker* Vol. 52/ 2 (Summer), 69-73.

Flynn, Laurie. 1979. "A Parent's Perspective." *Public Welfare* Vol. 37/3 (Summer) 28-33.

Garber, Ralph, D.S.W. 1985. "Disclosure of Adoption Information Report of the Special Commissioner to the Honourable John Sweeney, Minister of Community and Social Services, Government of Ontario."

Gediman, Judith S. and Brown, Linda P. 1989. *Birthbond: Reunions Between Birthparents & Adoptees — What Happens After....* Far Hills, New Jersey: New Horizon Press.

Gibb-Clark, Margot. 1985. "Getting Together After Adoption."*The Globe and Mail*, December 14.

Gibbs, Nancy. 1989. "The Baby Chase," *Time* October 9, 58-61.

The Globe and Mail. 1988. "When Adopted Children Seek Their Past," July 21.

Gonyo, Barbara. "Genetic Sexual Attraction."Prospect Heights, Illinois, Truth Seekers In Adoption,

Gritter, Jim. 1988 "Adoption's Dilemma: Dogs and Cats or Soup and Sandwich?" *Decree* (American Adoption Congress) Vol. 5/ 213,4,6.

Grof, Stanislav. 1988. *The Adventure of Self Discovery.* Albany, New York: State University of New York Press.

Hall, Joseph. 1992. "Man finds long lost brother—living in Joyceville prison." *The Toronto Star*, August 9.

Hormann, Elizabeth. 1987. *After the Adoption*. Old Tappan, New Jersey: Fleming H. Revell Company.

Kelly, John and Sanger, Sirgay, M.D. 1985. *You And Your Baby's First Year*. New York, New York: William Morrow and Company, Inc.

Lifton, Betty Jean. 1988. *Lost and Found*. New York: Harper and Row.

Marcus, Clare. 1979. *Adopted? A Canadian Guide for adopted adults in search of their origins*. Vancouver: International Self-Counsel Press Ltd.

MacArthur, Mary. 1990 "Parents lived nearby but son didn't know it." *The London Free Press*, May 16.

McColm, Michelle. 1990. "Mirror, Mirror on the wall..." *Encounter Magazine*, April 28, 3.

_____. 1989. "Family Reunion." *Perception Canada's Social Development Magazine* Vol.13/3, 10-13.

Meredith, Nikki. 1987. "Adoption can Be Tough for Child, Parents." *The Toronto Star*, May 8.

Mitchell Alanna. 1992. "Birth mother stays in touch." *The Globe and Mail*, November 30.

_____. 1992. "Newborns go with dollar flow." *The Globe and Mail*, November 30.

_____. 1992. "Private adoptions face few controls." *The Globe and Mail*, December,1.

_____. 1992. "Private system under spotlight." *The Globe and Mail*, December 2.

Pavao, Joyce Maguire. 1989. "A Study of the Themes that Appear in a Clinical Population of AdolescentAdoptees," Doctor of Education Thesis, Harvard University, Faculty of the Graduate

School of Education, Boston.

Redmond, Wendie, Sleightholm, Sherry. 1982. *Once Removed: Voices From Inside The Adoption Triangle*. Toronto: McGraw-Hill Ryerson Limited.

Riben, Marsha. 1988. *Shedding Light On The Dark Side of Adoption*. Detroit: Harlo Press.

Ruben, Suzanne. 1986. *Adoption: Beyond the Veil*. Los Angeles: Concerned United Birthparents (unpublished paper).

Sachdev, Paul, Ph.D. 1984. *Adoption: Current Issues and Trends*. Toronto and Vancouver: Butterworth & Co. (Canada) Ltd.

____. 1990. *Unlocking the Adoption Files*. New York: The Free Press.

Sanders, Patricia and Nancy Sitterly. 1981. *Search Aftermath and Adjustments*. Costa Mesa, California: ISC Publications.

Schaefer, Carol. 1991. *The Other Mother*. New York: Soho Press Inc.

Silverstein, Deborah with Sharon Kaplan. 1989. "Seven Core Issues in Adoption: A Therapeutic Framework." *Adopted Child* Vol 8/10 (October), 1-3.

Spencer, Phyllis. 1989. "The Gene Scene." *Encounter Magazine*, The London Free Press. January 28, 10,12.

Sorosky, Arthur D. M.D., Baran, Annette M.S.W., and Pannor, Reuben M.S.W. 1989. *The Adoption Triangle: Sealed or Opened Records: How They Affect Adoptees, Birth Parents, and Adoptive Parents*. San Antonio: Corona Publishing Co.

Vernon, P.A. 1987. "Western Ontario Adoption Project", ongoing study of adoptees and their birth families at the University of Western Ontario, London, Ontario.

Verny, Thomas, M.D. with John Kelly. 1981. *The Secret Life of the Unborn Child*. New York: Dell Publishing.

Verrier, Nancy, 1993. *The Primal Wound: Understanding the Adoptive Child*. Baltimore, MD: Gateway Press.